D0949588

Why Nationalism

Why

Nationalism

Yael Tamir

Princeton University Press
Princeton and Oxford

Published by Princeton University Press
41 William Street, Princeton, New Jersey 08540
6 Oxford Street, Woodstock, Oxfordshire OX20 1TR

press.princeton.edu

Library of Congress Control Number: 2018953761
ISBN 9780691190105

British Library Cataloging-in-Publication Data is available

Editorial: Rob Tempio and Matt Rohal
Production Editorial: Mark Bellis
Text Design: Leslie Flis
Jacket Design: Layla Mac Rory
Production: Jacqueline Poirier
Publicity: James Schneider
Copyeditor: Dawn Hall

This book has been composed in Arno Pro

Printed on acid-free paper. ∞

Printed in the United States of America

10 9 8 7 6 5 4 3 2 1

This book is dedicated
with much love and admiration
to my great teacher and mentor
Sir Isaiah Berlin

Contents

Foreword

Nationalism is one of those words that evokes a knee-jerk, invariably negative response in polite company. Associated with military aggression, genocide, and ethnic cleansing, it is tainted by the worst horrors of the twentieth century. Our present-day demagogues in the United States and Europe—Donald Trump, Marine Le Pen, Viktor Orban, and others—are further reinforcing this image by fanning the flames of nativism, xenophobia, and religious bigotry in its name.

Yael "Yuli" Tamir sees the destructive forces that nationalism can unleash. But she also sees something else that few liberals do these days: a modern democracy needs nationalism—or the nation-state—as much as it needs liberalism. As she explains in this fascinating book, decades of economic prosperity and apparent political consensus over liberal democratic principles have blinded us to the work nationalism was doing beneath the surface. Professor Tamir's bold thesis is that this work was, for the most part, constructive. The spread of economic opportunity, education, and political equality were all the products, she says, of an "alliance between the nation and the state." No institution has done better than the nation-state, and there are no alternatives yet in sight.

Bolder still is Yuli Tamir's call for a return to a nationalist ethos. Is "Putting America First?" a fascist slogan, she asks. Her answer: not necessarily. To be sure, she is not defending the xenophobic nativism of Donald Trump. Nationalism need not mean a sense of supremacy vis-à-vis other nations. It can serve instead "a desire to regenerate a sense of commitment among fellow nationals." Liberals must relearn the indispensable unifying role that a shared, cross-class cultural narrative plays.

The uncomfortable fact for many liberals and socialists alike is that "no social contract and no system of distribution can function as an open political framework"—that is, without borders and rules on who belongs, who doesn't. The nation and the state depend on each other. Tamir emphasizes here the cultural, psychological content of nationalism—the meaning-creation aspect that ties us to each other. I would emphasize equally the economic aspects. The nation, however constructed, needs the state to provide what an economist would call public goods—education, infrastructure, law and order. The state in turn needs the nation for legitimacy, interpersonal trust, and a sense of common fate.

The key question is: who are the people? Liberals and nationalists differ in what Tamir calls their "ethos of formation": nationalists stress history and fate while liberals believe in voluntarism. But, as she points out, true voluntarism is an option for only a lucky few. Only a tiny minority of skilled professionals and wealthy investors has the luxury to roam the world in pursuit of wider social networks and expanded economic opportunities. These cosmopolitan globalists—citizens of nowhere, in Theresa May's evocative language—have managed to revoke their responsibilities within their home nation without in fact taking on corresponding obligations anywhere else. The resulting economic and social polarization within nations makes it much more difficult to construct a "unifying narrative." With the elites having absconded thanks to globalization, the political playing field is now wide open for nativist extremists.

Tamir recognizes that nationalism can be exclusionary and turn nasty when it is coupled with violation of minority groups' rights. She argues that this can be overcome by accepting the right to be different and fostering empathy for citizens who are cultural outsiders. In the end, she acknowledges that her brand of nationalism is a compromise among liberal and national principles, an "untidy mix." What Tamir argues for, in the title of her earlier book, is liberal nationalism; hers is a conditional defense of nationalism.

Many liberals will no doubt think this goes too far toward glorifying some majority "identity" and "culture" at the expense of minorities. Still, they will have to answer the challenge Tamir has put to them. Xenophobia and nativism have little justification, but this does not mean that the demand for recognition and dignity of those left behind by neoliberal globalism is without moral value.

Like almost every ideology, nationalism can be taken in destructive or constructive directions. The great value of Tamir's book is to show us that there is indeed a positive direction. The book goes much beyond bowing to the obvious reality that the nation-state is back; it presents a principled case for why we need it politically. Tamir argues we can and must harness nationalism for the good of society. We better listen to her message before it is too late to fend off the extremists and save nationalism from the fascists.

Dani Rodrik

A Personal Note

I am a strange political creature; I have been a labor activist all my adult life, a fully committed human rights activist (one of the founders of the Israeli peace movement and for a while the chair of the Israeli Human Rights Association) and a liberal political theorist. In my private life I was fortunate enough to be somewhat of a global trotter. Hence it seemed only natural that I'd be a firm supporter of globalism and the set of values that comes with it: open borders, free trade, and free movement. But liberalism always seemed to me missing the human point. A political theory should be attuned to human needs and aspirations, and liberalism has been adjusting itself to a very particular kind of life experience.

It was probably my upbringing that made me attentive to national claims. For many years my pro-nationalism views were seen, at best, as irrelevant, a relic of a troubling past that should be transcendent. At times my academic friends turned a blind eye; at others they hoped I'd grow out of it. But when everybody was rejoicing the victory of liberalism I went the other way. Maybe because of my years in politics (serving in two Israeli governments, first as minister of immigration [1998–2001] and then as minister of education [2006–9]), I realized that the pull of the liberal argument was class-based—my class. I also followed, with great worry, the way members of other classes turned the other way. I could feel the earth trembling under liberal feet. It wasn't due to the well-orchestrated joy of the liberal victory party—it was because the liberal party was restricted in scope; though all my friends were attending, many stayed outside the fence.

In 2001 I ended a paper titled "Class and Nation" with the following words:

> Defensive-regressive nationalism threatens those who are eager to ride the waves of global open markets. For them nationalism is no more than a set of burdensome sentimental recollections, for all the rest it is still the most profitable socio-economic option. It is thus rational, for the immobile classes to try and force the mobile classes to participate in the nationalist game—they can easily be tempted to do so by exerting political pressures and quite often by means of social and political violence. When members of the mobile classes try, in order to loosen the social bonds, to either ignore or solve the conflict they are accused of non-patriotic tendencies. The class conflict has been translated into national terms.
>
> Marx was, then, wrong about the century in which class struggles will take place. If such struggles will erupt they will be in the twenty first century. And they will not feature the international solidarity of the proletariat. They will be struggles in which the immobile classes fight against each other as well against their own mobile elites. Members of the middle classes for whom globalization is no less threatening are likely to join the immobile, making them a social power that cannot be ignored.
>
> The workers of the world will never unite. They have no real interest to do so. Nationalism is therefore here to stay. Yet it might turn from the vision of the elites into their nightmare. It will join hands with every ideology that fosters closer and justifies exclusion. Xenophobic nationalism, the kind fostered by Le-Pan, Jorg Hider, the late Pim Fortuyn, by advocates of transfer policies in Israel as well as by supporters of White Australia or White California, will become more popular. It is not, however, as many have suspected, a nationalism driven by irrational forces. It is a rational nationalism

driven by the self-interest of the masses to protect them from a global dream they cannot share.

Can these developments be avoided or slowed down? The present global crisis provides an opportunity for change. The terrorist attack on September 11 made members of the mobile and affluent classes in America, and elsewhere, much more aware of their susceptibility to life-threatening risks. The present economic crisis makes them aware of their economic vulnerability. This may inspire, in the upper classes, a will to come back home in order to form a new "risk pool" which will defend their interests, as well as the interests of lower classes. If this will be the outcome of September 11th events then they will enhance national solidarity and delay the class struggle. If, however, the different classes keep marching on different routes, a moment of confrontation will arrive.[1]

Needless to say, in the seventeen years since 9/11, things haven't gotten any better; in fact, they have gotten worse. Many now realize it is time for change. This book is written with the hope that the present melancholy and sense of defeat among liberals will be replaced with a new political awareness that might lead to fresh political ideas and some better political arrangements.

In order for such changes to happen, liberals should acknowledge that their theoretical and political mistakes were grounded in a misinterpretation of one of the most basic notions of all—human freedom. Freedom was never just about the ability to move or trade freely; it was about the ability of individuals to govern their life, make meaningful choices, and live productively. For several decades liberals consistently ignored the fact that these kinds of freedoms were restricted not only by race or gender but also by transgenerational poverty associated with one's place of birth. The marginalization of class talk and the reluctance to turn the fight against poverty into a major motivational political force channeled the liberal progressive debate away from questions that are relevant to the sinking middle. Members of the middle classes thus lost trust in the ruling liberal elites and questioned their willingness to protect the interests of the different social classes.

We are therefore facing a unique historical moment characterized by a decline in social trust and the erosion of liberal-progressive leadership. Liberal democrats are asked to answer questions typical of constitutive moments: Who are we? What defines our common political identity? Why should we trust one another? And how can we work together to create a safer future? Unfortunately, they have no adequate answers.

Nationalism has a long tradition of answering these same questions, and it is therefore back, yet without the balancing power of liberalism and democracy it can easily turn destructive. In order to prevent it from going astray, the three-way partnership among nationalism, liberalism, and democracy must be renewed. It has given the twentieth century some of its finest hours and could become the savior of the twenty-first century. The much-discussed crisis of modern democracies is inherently associated with the breakdown of this partnership. Democracy cannot be restored as a purely utilitarian project, only as a national one—as a framework that provides meaning and reasons for mutual care and responsibility. Self-centered individualism must therefore be replaced with a more collectivist spirit that nationalism knows how to kindle. This book is an attempt to offer a middle ground that can restore the power of the nation-state, making it more profitable for the many, not only for the few.

Part I

The Return of History

Hope is certainly not the same thing as optimism. It is not the conviction that something will turn out well, but the certainty that something makes sense regardless of how it turns out.

VACLAV HAVEL, *DISTURBING THE PEACE* (1986)

1

The New Nationalism

It has been a long time since streets were crowded with people waving national flags; now people are marching all over the globe: in Barcelona, Britain, Austria, and France, in the main streets of Kurdistan, in the United States, and in the public squares of Istanbul. Flag waving for and against political causes is back in fashion. Nationalism is everywhere.

The reemergence of nationalism has taken the world by surprise. This was supposed to be a liberal and democratic century; history was about to end and the flat world promised to bring the inhabitants of the globe closer together. Liberals believed that their century (starting from 1945) would see the end of wars, the spread of reason, and the beginning of a new enlightenment. This vision captivated the imagination, promising endless economic growth, expanding opportunities, and an ongoing increase in well-being. Each generation was to be better off than its predecessors.

Disappointingly, the twenty-first century opened with a series of social and economic crises. Many of the achievements of the previous decades have come under threat; the young generations fear the return of the crisis of capitalism and worry about the well-being of their parents and their children. No wonder that liberal optimism has lost its popularity and that those who several years ago chanted "Yes, We Can!" now suspect "we" cannot.

Trump's election alongside Brexit, the growing support for separatist movements, the rise of the new right in many European countries, and the phenomena of national and religious awakenings around the world leave liberals perplexed. They were convinced they were doing the right thing. Michael Moore proudly summarized their achievements:

> Things are better. The left has won the cultural wars. Gays and lesbians can get married. A majority of Americans now take the liberal position on just about every polling question posed to them: Equal pay for women—check. Abortion should be legal—check. Stronger environmental laws—check. More gun control—check. Legalize marijuana—check.[1]

One day, on his way home, Moore was stopped by a man who said: "Mike . . . we have to vote for Trump. We HAVE to shake things up." Why did he say that? The man's words made Moore stop and think. This is the virtue of many of the recent political events; they force us to stop and reflect on the way we have interpreted the basic social and economic developments of the last half of a century.

Historical turning points are difficult to detect—usually they are acknowledged in retrospect; the assassination of Archduke Franz Ferdinand of Austria in Sarajevo, the self-immolation of an unknown Tunisian street merchant, and the first inflatable boat loaded with refugees crossing the Mediterranean changed the world, yet it took some time before the massive scope of the change was acknowledged. We tend to analyze events in hindsight. Why did the people revolt? Why did the refuges start to flee across the Mediterranean at a certain point in time? Why didn't the man share Moore's view that things are so much better? Much of this book is an answer to these questions, yet unlike many commentators who put the blame on those who acted against their expectations, I ask a different question: why were the accumulating warning signs that the social and political crisis is deepening transparent to those in power? The blindness I am interested in is that of the elites.

The present political upheaval is a necessary wake-up call, an invitation to admit that the liberal-progressive camp has made its mistakes and must look back on the last forty years with a sense of self-criticism. Many would like to think that the present state of affairs is no more than a sad coincidence; that things could easily have gone the other way, and soon they would go back to normal. They are wrong. Among Trump's tweets, Le Pen's slogans, and the demonstrations of the extreme right, some real concerns are hidden. It is dangerous to comfort oneself with the fact that actually Hillary won the popular vote, Le Pen wasn't elected, and Brexit supporters did not know what the European Union was all about and now regret their vote. Whether winning or losing, new powers entered the political game, and they cannot be ignored.

In liberalism's victorious years the Western world assumed it had outgrown nationalism; now that it is back it lacks the tools to accommodate its challenge. Why nationalism now? What provoked national feelings and national ideology and made them more relevant than ever? Is nationalism a dormant evil force waiting to pop out whenever there is a crisis, a force that must be repressed at all costs, or is it a constructive power, a worthwhile ideology that could and should be harnessed to make the world a better place? This book presents a case for nationalism, highlighting the ways it shaped public policy and made the years between the end of the world wars and the eruption of neoliberal globalism the best years for the least well-off members of the developed world.[2] Some may say that these years were good ones because nationalism was repressed, allowing liberal democracy to flourish. I, however, wish to argue the opposite—namely, that many of the achievements of that period were dependent on an alliance between the nation and the state.

True, neither liberals nor nationalists are eager to expose their interdependencies—as with many odd couples, they wish to distance themselves, avoiding the embarrassment associated with admitting they cannot do without each other. But they have been partners for years. The vigor and anger with which liberals are rejecting nationalism are not a sign of estrangement but a cover-up of a too-intimate reliance.

Political ideologies would like to be self-sufficient; they tremble at the thought of their shortcomings being exposed. I wish to do exactly that—expose the ideological interdependencies that shape our world, arguing that the modern democratic state cannot have survived without the supportive hand of both liberal and national ideologies. My argument highlights areas where liberal democratic theory draws on national criteria to counter the pressures of globalism, and where nationalism relies on liberal-democratic principles to strengthen its claims for self-determination.

The nation-state has been an ideal meeting point between the two, and hence it is here to stay. Democratic regimes require a pre-political partnership that turns citizens into a collective entity that has a common past and a common future. In the absence of a political *we*, states disintegrate, and the political structure that allows them to turn into democratic and decent entities dissolves.

A political *we* had never been a natural phenomenon; it must be created, and then constantly nurtured, supported, and reinvented. This is an old truth that is easily forgotten. States are manmade entities that need to be cherished and maintained. Enchanted with what seemed to be their conclusive victory, liberal democracies felt secure and ignored the ongoing work of state building. Confident that they would last forever, they neglected the need for ideological and political maintenance. They withdrew from the public sphere, became reluctant to nurture a unifying cultural and political narrative that acculturates citizens to confront the evolving social and economic conditions. Invisible hands were expected to solve social problems and merge the different identities gathered under the wings of the Rainbow Coalition into a new social identity strong enough to carry the burden of the state. No wonder states are now facing an existential crisis.

While liberal democrats were paralyzed by their assumed victory, nationalists felt defeated and obsolete. In most of the developed world they were taken to be outdated, carrying the voice of political immaturity, raising the kind of ideas civilized people don't mention around a dinner table. They have therefore lost the ability to offer the state a supportive hand.

With no one working to preserve its unique structure, the modern nation-state started crumbling down. Should we lament its disintegration? Many argue that nowadays it is more of a burden than an asset; that it fitted the needs of modernization but that it cannot meet the needs of a postindustrial world, that we should let it be torn apart by global and local forces and opt for a better alternative—yet none has so far emerged.

The present social and political chaos exposes the damaging outcomes of the theoretical and political void caused by the demise of the nation-state. When states step aside they leave behind a social, political, economic, and cultural vacuum. The public sphere is emptied of ideological and motivational forces that could promote social solidarity and encourage the erection of mechanisms necessary to combat growing social alienation.

Even when state intervention is indispensable, the language used to justify it has been delegalized; national planning is assumed to be breeding inefficiency and corruption, undermining the productive spirit kindled by personal freedom. In time, resentment of the state crossed party lines, joining liberals and conservatives in a struggle for personal freedom. This led to the shrinking of the state and the erosion of its regulatory powers. Checks and balances were removed, allowing markets to shape public life. The weakness of the state alongside the prominence of the markets opened unprecedented opportunities for a new kind globalism that is individualistic rather than state governed. Each person was encouraged to compete on his/her own. In an age marked by competitiveness, people are ready to do "whatever it takes" to have the upper hand. They compete internally and internationally without ever thinking of the larger social effects of their actions. As a result, social and economic gaps grow, and the social contract held by a combination of democratic and national beliefs loses its power. With the spreading of social disarray, some political players try to capture the opportunity and draft a new contract that would serve their interests. Seeking to justify their claims they turn to nationalism—which in modern times was, and still is, the greatest legitimizing political power.

Present-day nationalism appears in two different forms, both grounded in the weakness of the state: the first, the more classic one, is to be found in Catalonia, Lombardy, and Vento as well as in Flanders, Transylvania, Scotland, Kurdistan, and lately Brazil. It represents the desire of national groups, concentrated in distinct territories, to capture the opportunity and demand self-rule. As this claim is voiced in the name of the people, such national movements try to recruit as many fellow nationals as possible. Consequently, they are inwardly inclusive, bringing on board each and every member of the nation regardless of age, gender, or class, nurturing a partnership among the elites, the middle classes, and the working classes to back the national agenda.

Separatist national movements challenge the boundaries of existing states for both national and economic reasons. Often they represent the desire of the more affluent regions to be freed from the obligation to share their wealth with members of poorer regions they now take to be outsiders. The affluent attempt to rewrite the political contract in ways that will secure them better life chances, offering new political and cultural opportunities to their elites and a larger share of the national wealth to the people.

The second kind of nationalism is the nationalism of the less well-off, those left defenseless by the process of hyperglobalization.[3] The vulnerable revoke national feelings in order to convince the elites to come back home from their global voyage and put their nation first. Because the vulnerable do not inhabit a defined territory or have a distinct identity, they define themselves in opposition to others. From here, the distance to an aggressive, xenophobic type of nationalism is short. Yet, despite their brutal language and their association with hateful right-wing movements, many of the claims the vulnerable make are not without moral value. The demand to rewrite the social contract in ways that will answer their needs is a legitimate one. Their request to be included and fairly treated is as justified as their xenophobia is morally unwarranted.

The nationalism of the vulnerable is a revolt against the betrayal of the global elites. The vulnerable rightly feel it is unjust that those who exploit cheap labor and natural resources overseas are allowed to portray themselves as moral universalists, while those trying to defend their jobs and their future back home are labeled as narrow-minded bigots. They would like their claims to be taken seriously rather than rejected offhand, dismissed as populists or reactionaries.

Liberals would like us to believe that nationalists are morally inferior to globalists. They conveniently ignore the strong correlation between social class and political preferences. Some suggest that this correlation attests to the fact that moral and political competence varies among members of the different social classes, or to put it bluntly, that the more educated and affluent exercise better judgment than the rest. My theory travels between the two types of nationalism, making it harder to pin nationalism on the hillbillies, the rednecks, or European right-wing extremists. The savvy people of Catalan and northern Italy force us to think harder about the origins of nationalism and its role in the contemporary political reality.

It is easier to be a globalist if you are likely to enjoy the benefits of an open market, or to support free immigration if you feel secure in your social status and do not fear that newcomers are going to take your job, or reduce the value of your property by renting the next-door apartment, forcing your neighborhood schools to face new challenges. Likewise, it is logical to be against separatism if you think you might be on the losing side and support it if you expect to enjoy its benefits. This means that moral and social luck plays an important role in determining the scope of values and behaviors individuals are likely to consider and are able to endorse.[4] If one's position in the national-global debate strongly correlates to one's actual interests and expectations, there is no reason to describe one side as being more rational, moral, or open-minded than the other. Exposing the rational aspects hidden in national choices, and contrary to most commentators, I suggest that the reemergence of national feelings is a sensible response to the present social, political, and economic circumstances rather than an uncontrolled outburst of destructive human qualities.

Nationalism has always been part of the modern political world, at times occupying the back seat, at others the front row. The persistence of nationalism attests to its inherent value. This book aims to enumerate the assets that nationalism brings to the political discourse and examine a variety of national claims without falling into the ad hominem trap of rebutting ideas by attacking the people making the argument or those associated with them. The present political discourse deals far too often with the (problematic) personalities of the deliverers rather than with the issues themselves. It is therefore important to emphasize that what follows is not an argument in support of any particular leader or political movement but an examination of the accuracy of theoretical claims judged on their own merit.

The text tries to keep a calm tone, avoiding the hysteria or melancholia characteristic of present-day political exchanges; it takes a step back in order to get some perspective and encourage intellectual modesty so desperately needed these days. In this spirit it shuns inflated declarations and false promises and tries to adjust expectations to the social and political conditions of our time. Much of the present-day sense of disappointment is grounded in the inability of both theorists and political leaders to break away from the illusion that all problems can be solved, that progress is eternal and there will be more for everyone.

It's not without hesitation that I set out to write this text. Taking a pro-nationalist view one faces a risk that some arguments will be used to support unworthy policies. But the fear of being used should not stop one from drawing attention to some valid arguments.

Things are likely to get tougher in years to come, and without human empathy and national solidarity there is no way forward. What is desperately needed is a Churchill who will not promise greatness or togetherness but "blood, toil, tears, and sweat," or a Roosevelt who will urge people not to fear but to support "a leadership of frankness and of vigor" that will encourage nations to build a bearable future.

Intellectual history resembles an archaeological mount built from remnants of great ideas. In order to move to a new era one needs to dig in, brush off the dust, examine the way ideas were used in order to build a theory that is, at the same time, new and familiar. Liberalism with its faults and virtues, democracy with its promise of self-rule, national ideology with its transgenerational communal aspirations, and class-related theories with their sensitivity to the way social status dictates one's life options must be included. From the theoretical fragments of the last century a new theory should be built that fits the needs of the twenty-first century.[5]

2

Never Say Never

On November 11, 1918, World War I came to an end. Over sixteen million people were killed in a war described as the war to end all wars. Seeking ways to ensure an everlasting peace, the League of Nations was created. Revulsion with war and futile bloodshed was a popular sentiment in the 1920s. Nothing describes it better than Erich Maria Remarque's *All Quiet on the Western Front*. The book tells the story of a generation of men who were destroyed by the war and criticizes the detachment of the decision makers, far removed from the horrors of the front, condemning people to death without caring to know who they were. After years of fighting in the trenches, Paul, the book's hero, is killed: "He fell in October 1918, on a day that was so quiet and still on the whole front, that the army report confined itself to the single sentence: All quiet on the Western front."[1]

By the end of World War I, nationalism was on the winning side. Woodrow Wilson's Fourteen Points as well as Lenin's support for national self-determination made national policies the guiding principle of the new world order. In the first wave of national self-determination twenty-six new states were born and more were soon to follow.

The national spring and the hopes for eternal peace ended exactly twenty years later in March 1938 with the Anschluss—the annexation of Austria to Nazi Germany—and with Neville Chamberlain signing the Treaty of Munich promising "peace for our time." In 1939 World War II erupted; it was longer and dead-lier than the first. It lasted six years and a day and left behind an unprecedented number of casualties: over seventy million dead and hundreds of millions injured and displaced.

In the West, the liberating perception of nationalism was re-placed with a demonic one. Nationalism came to be seen as a vile force that sets free the evil that lies within us. Nazism showed that even the most cultured of all nations, "the land of the poets and thinkers" (*Das Land der Dichter und Denker*), wears its humanis-tic values lightly only to cover a deep-rooted dark spirit. Neither culture nor philosophy could stop Hitler and his troops. While German elites were reading Kant's "Perpetual Peace" and venerating universal brotherhood, they were ordering the per-secution and extermination of entire peoples. One particular moment captures the bitter irony of this situation. The movie *The Reichsorchester*, which tells the story of the Berlin philharmonic orchestra, opens with a scene from a ceremonial concert that took place in 1942. In the spectacular concert hall, crowded with cultured music lovers, Joseph Goebbels, Hitler's minister of pro-paganda, sang the praise of the Führer before introducing the musical pieces. Then, the orchestra played and the choir sang Friedrich Schiller's "Ode to Joy," a part of Beethoven's Ninth Symphony: "Your magic joins again. What convention strictly divides; All people become brothers . . . You millions I embrace you. This kiss is for all the world." The gas chambers at Auschwitz were already releasing clouds of human smoke; the generals humming Schiller's words were fueling these chambers. It thus became clear that being culturally savvy was not enough to evoke a commitment to universal human values. The most cultural and abysmal of human experiences could live not only within one nation but also within one person. For more than eight years Europe sank into a moral abyss.

When the war was finally over, optimism resurfaced. Repressing the horrors of the war and forgetting the ease with which people had been recruited to join the ranks of the executioners allowed confidence in the benevolence of humanity to be regained. Nationalism, it was assumed, had been defeated forever. In his informative book *Year Zero: A History of 1945*, Ian Buruma describes the first New Year's Eve in Berlin after the end of the war:

> Some were chanting: "*Wir Sind das Volk!*" ("We are the people!"). Others sang: "We are one people!" But there was nothing nationalistic or menacing in the air of that night. It was an international crowd, a kind of political Woodstock without rock bands, celebrating freedom, togetherness, and hope for a better world, in which the bitter experiences of the past would not be repeated; no more barbed wire, or camps, or killing. It was good to be young. If ever Beethoven's anthem of "All Men Will Be Brothers" ("*Alle Menschen werden Bruder*") had meaning, it was on that extraordinary New Year's Eve in Berlin.[2]

After the war, nationalism was discredited in the West, dissociated from its liberal foundations and associated with murderous totalitarianism. It did, however, keep its liberating power in the developing world and was the engine behind postcolonial movements.[3] In many ways this division between the developed world, which was supposed to have moved beyond nationalism, and the developing world, which was just growing into its national stage, reflected the liberal theory of human progress: nationalism was a necessary though not a final stage of moral and political development. While essential in moments of political birth, in maturity nationalism must be transcendent, giving way to universalism.

Less than ten years after the end of the war, it was clear that a new front was opened. The enemies of the West were now living in Moscow, threatening to bring liberal democracies to an end. Senator McCarthy was hunting down Communists all over America. In October 1957 the Soviet Union launched Sputnik into orbit: "The Sputnik's radio signal highlighted not only the fact that the Soviet Union had beaten the United States into space, it also made it clear the Soviets possessed rocket technology strong enough to launch nuclear bombs at the United States."[4] The Sputnik's beeping signal stimulated a wave of American nationalism and led to reforms in science and engineering education to enable America to regain its technological and national prominence.

From the assassination of Martin Luther King to the students' marches in Europe, 1968 seemed, once again, a turning point. The anti–Vietnam War demonstrations that started in the United States spread to London, Paris, and Berlin; the civil rights and human rights movements gathered support; and youth culture exploded with force. On the eve of his assassination, King delivered an inspiring and uplifting speech that would define the American progressive vision, a fine combination of liberal and national values, connecting the love of country (its topography affectionately depicted) and the love of human kind.

> And if America is to be a great nation, this must become true. And so let freedom ring from the prodigious hilltops of New Hampshire. Let freedom ring from the mighty mountains of New York. Let freedom ring from the heightening Alleghenies of Pennsylvania. Let freedom ring from the snow-capped Rockies of Colorado. Let freedom ring from the curvaceous slopes of California. But not only that: Let freedom ring from Stone Mountain of Georgia. Let freedom ring from Lookout Mountain of Tennessee. Let freedom ring from every hill and molehill of Mississippi. From every mountainside, let freedom ring.

Freedom was not only an American dream. In 1968 Czech president Alexander Dubček tried to convince the Soviet leadership to award his country independence. He pleaded for an alliance grounded in mutual national respect. The Soviet Union, he argued, should fully respect the sovereign rights of the Czech people. This acknowledgment is the sole "reliable basis for the further development of friendly relations."[5] His request was rejected, the Soviet army invaded Prague, and the tensions between the East and West reached a new peak. Jan Palach's act of self-immolation sent a clear message to the world that freedom is worth dying for. Yet, the Kremlin turned a blind eye. The USSR seemed an unshakable power.

Barely twenty years later, the Berlin Wall was demolished and the Soviet Union had collapsed. This was misguidedly taken as evidence of the end of all ideological struggles. In a dismissive tone Francis Fukuyama declared that socialism may still have "some isolated true believers left in places like Managua, Pyongyang, or Cambridge, Massachusetts,"[6] but globally it has lost its power. As liberalism declared its final triumph, Fukuyama was to announce victory:

> What we may be witnessing is not just the end of the Cold War, or the passing of a particular period of post-war history, but the end of history as such: that is, the end point of mankind's ideological evolution and the universalization of Western liberal democracy as the final form of human government.[7]

In the twentieth century, Fukuyama argued, "liberalism contended first with the remnants of absolutism, then Bolshevism and Fascism, and finally an updated Marxism that threatened to lead to the ultimate apocalypse of nuclear war. The struggle is now over."[8]

The great liberal enthusiasm overshadowed the fact that the collapse of the Soviet Union evoked national aspirations: within three years (1990–92) nineteen new states were established, all gaining their independence on grounds of national self-determination. In the eight months between May and December 1991, ten new states were established: Somaliland (May 18, 1991), Estonia (August 20, 1991), Ukraine (August 24, 1991), Moldova (August 27, 1991), Uzbekistan (September 1, 1991), Macedonia (September 8, 1991), Tajikistan (September 9, 1991), Croatia (October 8, 1991), Azerbaijan (October 18, 1991), and Kazakhstan (December 16, 1991). This was the second great wave of national liberation, yet it did not undermine the celebratory liberal spirit. On the contrary, the national aspect of the emergence of the new states was silenced, their establishment was taken as evidence of the victory of liberalism over communism.

The fact that in 1993 the European Union was established was taken to be the final proof that the West was approaching a post-national age. Ironically The European Union chose Hitler's beloved musical piece, played on his birthday—"Ode to Joy"—as its hymn, proving the shortness of human memory or maybe the victory of hope over experience.

Nationalism wasn't the only ideological power whose premature death has been announced. The events of 9/11 made it clear that religious fundamentalism was back. With the villains in the movies now speaking Arabic, the Western world met radical Islam. Only one ideology seemed uncheckable: capitalism. The second part of the twentieth century saw an amazing economic and political growth. With the help of the United States, Europe was rising out of the ashes to rebuild itself at an unprecedented speed. This process was to be seen as the beginning of a new age of endless progress.

Globalization was the vehicle by which liberalism expanded its ideology. All seemed well and quiet on the Western front until in 2001 Enron, one of the world's major electricity and natural gas corporations, collapsed and became the symbol of corporate corruption. The closing monologue of a play based on its collapse is delivered by Jeremy Skilling, Enron's CEO:

> I'm not a bad man. I'm not an unusual man. I just wanted to change the world. . . . I know it's hard to understand. . . . Everything I've ever done in my life worth anything has been done in a bubble; in a state of extreme hope and trust and stupidity. . . . Mark Twain once said: "Don't part with your illusions. When they are gone you may still exist, but you have ceased to live."[9]

By 2008 major cracks in the success story of neoliberalism started to appear. The stock exchange bubble burst and everybody was wondering how they hadn't seen it coming. On September 14, 2008, the American investment bank Lehman Brothers Holdings announced bankruptcy and the economic crisis went into full swing, and yet the supremacy of liberalism as the leading ideology didn't come into question. Or maybe it did: that same year, on August 8, an event took place the political importance of which went almost unnoticed: the Olympic Games opened in Beijing, sending an official announcement of the arrival of a new global superpower. In a traditional national manner, the opening ceremony created a continuous narrative, connecting China's glorious historical achievements to the present-day process of intense economic progress.[10] In the next ten years the promise made in the opening of the games was fulfilled and China became a major global power. In an interesting change of roles, it became the defender of globalism against its new rival, the United States. It is President Xi who now claims to defend free trade as part of his "One Belt, One Road" policy, while President Trump makes antiglobalism a centerpiece of his policies.

Xi's globalism is a nationalist one, a state-centered globalism, a version of globalism the West has surrendered. Xi never meant to allow the individualization of globalism; he remains within the centralist Chinese tradition but with an eye open to the world. Processes of globalization in the West were different. The move from state globalism to individual globalism had brutal outcomes for the developed world; the most of obvious was the collapse of middle classes and the rapid growth of social and economic gaps. No wonder those harmed by this stage of globalism are wishing to turn the clock back. This became evident in the debate over Brexit that placed EU supporters and globalists on the one side and nationalists on the other. We know who won the debate. Euro-skepticism and global skepticism is now spreading around the world. Citizens want to put their country first—and they have a good reason to demand we take their preferences seriously.

A hundred years of an ideological journey that has known unprecedented peaks and valleys ended in 2018. Starting with the "war to end all wars" and culminating in the "end of history," it was closed with the reemergence of nationalism, Brexit, and a wave of separatist demands. The losing ideologies are back, fighting for their position in the front; the winning ones are on the defense. If there is a lesson to be learned from the last hundred years, it is that nothing ends or begins as abruptly as it seems. Ideologies don't die out or disappear; they put on new garments, some makeup, adopt new slogans, and come back in a new guise. Ideological debates are, therefore, here to stay.

It is for the reader to decide whether this is good or bad news. It certainly reassures political theorists that in the foreseeable future they will not be out of work. A time-worn Jewish story summarizes their situation well. A man comes to the rabbi looking for a job. The rabbi suggests he should sit at the nearest crossroads. "And what will I do?" asks the man. "You will wait for the Messiah, and when he comes make sure he doesn't skip over our little town." "And how much will I earn?" "The pay," says the rabbi, "is modest but the job is permanent."

3

Untidy Compromises

The history of the last century teaches us that in the ideological world there are few victories and defeats; as circumstances change, ideas plunge and surface. A captivating image of this reality is offered by Michael Freeden,[1] who uses the analogy of pieces of furniture arranged in a room, each time in a different order according to the owner's taste. At times, freedom or autonomy occupy the central space, at others they are shoved to the background, replaced by other ideas like solidarity or community. Some balance between the old and the new will save us from making the most dangerous mistake of all: taking ideas, attractive as they may be, to their logical ends, or, to carry on the analogy, emptying the room of all but one kind of furniture.

One of the purposes of this book is to remind ourselves that one-sided political theories are bound to lead to moral and political calamities and to encourage a search for a set of compromises that fit the needs of our age.[2] We have a lot to learn from the failures and successes of the last century; the most important lesson of all is to be more critical of our own beliefs and more open to those of others. In what follows, two of the leading ideologies of the last century, liberal democracy and nationalism, are reviewed; from each of them, worthwhile human values and social strategies are exerted. Neither is dismissed by identifying it with its most extreme expressions: brutal neoliberalism on the one hand, Nazism and fascism on the other.

Balancing different ideas is a necessary moral and political skill. In the wise words of Sir Isaiah Berlin, given the variety of human needs that pull in different directions, the only way forward is by constantly searching for:

> some logically untidy, flexible, and even ambiguous compromise. Every situation calls for its own specific policy, since out of the crooked timber of humanity, as Kant once remarked, no straight thing was ever made. What the age calls for is not (as we are often told) more faith, or stronger leadership, or more scientific organization. Rather it is the opposite—less Messianic ardor, more enlightened skepticism, more toleration of idiosyncrasies, more frequent ad hoc measures to achieve aims in a foreseeable future, more room for attainment of their personal ends by individuals and by minorities whose tastes and beliefs find (whether rightly or wrongly must not matter) little response among the majority.[3]

Political theory seeks bearable, livable concessions. This is why political deliberations are so important. They provide us with an opportunity to think and act, allowing for active social and political participation. If no one true answer could be revealed by either rational deliberation or religious epiphany, political freedom is essential. We must therefore keep engaging with a wide range of worthwhile ideas drawn from different (sometimes conflicting) political theories, borrowing from each of them valuable insights and words of caution, thus creating a sphere of common discourse from which a more balanced set of practices can emerge.

Many may wonder: should nationalism be included in this balancing act? In order to answer this question I draw out some of the valuable and constructive aspects of nationalism, arguing that they reflect a scope of human needs and aspirations that should be considered. I do not attempt to beautify nationalism; I am well aware of its harmful aspects and destructive powers (much has been written on these issues, and readers can find a better analysis elsewhere). In this text I wish to present the case for nationalism, trying to highlight its importance in any future social construct.

Like every other idea, nationalism can be pulled in different directions. At its worst it has a devastating and destructive power; at its best, it is one of the most constructive and creative political forces. We should then try and benefit, as much as possible, from the national experience while keeping our eyes wide open to the risks that lie ahead. My defense of nationalism is therefore conditional, but political theory misses a lot when out of fear of the extreme it ignores ideas essential for our collective future.

Why nationalism now? In the developed world two related processes transformed the social and political landscape: the political pendulum swung too far to the individualist pole, leaving behind generations suffering from social alienation and anonymity, while the economic balance tilted too far to the free-market side, leaving too many individuals vulnerable. These transformations raise new challenges and call for new responses.

Political theory asks eternal questions, but its answers are context related. As the great American philosopher John Rawls taught us, even behind the "veil of ignorance" individuals must know general facts about their society. They must:

> understand political affairs and the principles of economic theory; know the basis of social organization and the law of human psychology. Indeed the parties are presumed to know whatever general facts affect the choice of the principles of justice.[4]

What are these facts? What are the basic organizing principles of our society? Was the last half decade one of progress or regress? There is no lack of facts, yet we look at these facts through an ideological and institutional prism. While many are now captivated with the issue of "fake news" and "fact checking," it is difficult to admit that some of the most basic social and economic facts remain contestable, and that some of the most firm political debates are grounded in our inability to agree on a description of the present state of affairs. With this remark in mind it may be less obvious who is a reactionary and who is a social critic.

The two kinds of nationalism presented in this book challenge the present political paradigms and dare to demand that we revisit the facts we know, as we have followed a one-sided interpretation of the social and economic developments. One of the chapters in Joseph E. Stiglitz's book *The Price of Inequality: How Today's Divided Society Endangers Our Future*[5] is captivatingly titled "1984 Is Upon Us." In clear prose Stiglitz demonstrates how the 1 percent has used its advantages "to alter perceptions and achieve its aim—to make our inequality less than it is and more acceptable than it should be." This is well known to anyone who ever read Marx or Gramsci; the ruling classes control not only the material means of production but also the intellectual ones, allowing them to present their positions as a universal truth. The social and political outcomes of intentional misrepresentation of facts are often devastating. Many of the recent events that took the world by surprise could have been prevented if the accumulating evidence refuting the ruling paradigm would have been more thoroughly evaluated.

It takes disruptive moments like the one we live in to force individuals to examine the match between their social conceptions and the present social and economic actualities and rethink their beliefs. It's time for political theory to admit that reality developed in surprising ways, hence the terms of the social and political debate must be altered, justice lies no longer on one side of the theoretical fence, and different voices must be given a place around the discussion table.

4

The Two Faces of Janus

Nationalism is a deceptive ideology; one of its faces looks to the past, the other looks to the future. Hence, the tendency to identify nationalism solely with reactionary views, overlooking its modernizing and liberating powers, represents a deep misunderstanding of the modern world, or maybe it's no more than a polemic stand meant to debunk nationalism, pushing it out of the political playing field.

Negative descriptions of nationalism that emphasize its backward-looking face are very common: Karl Popper described nationalism as a regressive force, a revolt against the open society, an emotive power that "appeals to our tribal instincts, to passion and to prejudice, and to our nostalgic desire to be relieved from the strain of individual responsibility which it attempts to replace by a collective or group responsibility."[1]

Indeed, nationalism often tries to revive (or invent) an image of a magnificent past. Seeing the past in all its splendor, Marc Lilla argues, places the reactionary "in a stronger position than his adversary because he believes he is the guardian of what actually happened, not the prophet of what might be. . . . And the reactionaries of our time have discovered that nostalgia can be a powerful political motivator perhaps even more powerful than hope. Hope can be disappointed. Nostalgia is irrefutable."[2]

While this may be a good definition of reactionaries, one must be careful not to conflate a criticism of the present with a desire to go back to some imaginary glorious past. Criticizing the current social order, claiming that some things have gone fundamentally wrong or worked better in the past, isn't necessarily nostalgia; it can be a mere fact. Describing a certain trend of social criticism as nostalgia is tantamount to dismissing it without ever examining the content of its claims. This is particularly problematic when the dismissal is voiced by those who benefit from the present state of affairs rather than by those who are harmed by it.

Despite its conservative image, when examining the history of nationalism, one of its most fascinating features is its modernizing powers. The basic characteristic of the modern nation and everything connected with it, writes Eric Hobsbawm in the preface to his seminal book on nationalism, "is its modernity."[3] He goes on to argue that at the end of the nineteenth century and the beginning of the twentieth the only historically justifiable nationalism was that which fitted with progress that "enlarged rather than restricted the scale on which human economies, societies and cultures operated."[4]

Ernest Gellner, another highly regarded scholar of nationalism, makes a similar claim:

> Nationalism is not the awakening of an old, latent, dormant force, though that is how it does indeed present itself. It is in reality the consequence of a new form of social organization, based on deeply internalized, education-dependent high culture, each protected by its own state.[5]

Despite its romantic and nostalgic appearance, he adds, nationalism is integral to modernity and progress; it was born in the bosom of the industrial society, which is

> the only society ever to live by and rely on sustained and perpetual growth, on an expected and continuous improvement. Not

surprisingly, it was the first society to invent the concept and ideal of progress. . . . Many societies in the past have on occasion discovered innovations and improved their lot, and sometimes it may even be true that improvements came not as single spies but in battalions. But the improvement was never perpetual, never expected to be so.[6]

In her important book *Nationalism: Five Roads to Modernity*, Liah Greenfeld makes the most radical claim regarding the connection between nationalism and modernity. The nation, she argues, is the constitutive element of modernity. "Rather than define nationalism by its modernity, I see modernity as defined by nationalism."[7]

It is therefore safe to conclude that despite the common perception of nationalism as identified with primordial, tribal feelings, the true power of nationalism in modern times is grounded in its ability to promote processes of modernization and industrialization that go hand in hand with the universalization of education, information, and technology. Although it was the most efficient agent of modernization, nationalism managed to present social and political change as an expression of fate and continuity. The move toward the future was to be seen as an extension of the past, change and mobility as a stroll within the old family yard. Never was a mobilizing ideology marketed in such gentle and comforting tones, pleasing to the ears of those members of society for whom change and uncertainty seem a frightening prospect. Nationalism not only helped the process of political modernization, it also answered the needs of the modern mind. To begin with, it is grounded in concepts such as self-rule and self-expression. Emperors and kings expect their subjects to be obedient; democrats demand that they become active political agents; nationalists aspire to induce in them the will to use cultural and creative tools to express themselves in both the private and the public sphere. The modern nation-state thus invited individuals to partake in the political, ethical, and cultural sphere. Its goals were forward looking; when it looked back to the past, it did so in order to set goals for the future. In Nietzsche's words, the vision of the past is used to kindle in individuals "the hope that justice will yet come and happiness is behind the mountain they are climbing. They believe that the meaning of existence will become ever clearer in the course of its evolution, they only look backward at the process to understand the present and stimulate their longing for the future." Nietzsche understood well the motivating power of a past constructed and made fit to produce a prototype for the future. History is an activating power, and nationalism made good use of this quality in harnessing individuals to its social and political goals. Identifying nationalism with a reactionary spirit is therefore a basic misunderstanding rather than a descriptive claim; it is a normative statement meant to conceal nationalism's mobilizing powers.

Another way of dismissing nationalism is by portraying it as an expression of a populist state of mind. Populism is such a vague term that it can be applied to a wide range of political movements. Despite their many differences, both the Tea Party and Occupy Wall Street are considered to be populist movements. No wonder that in 2017 the Cambridge Dictionary declared populism the word of the year, describing it as a set of "political ideas and activities that are intended to get the support of ordinary people by giving them what they want."

The dictionary further claims that people tend to use the term with reference to "the implied lack of critical thinking on the part of the populace, and the implied cynicism on the part of the leaders who exploit it." In other words, populism is a political ploy to mobilize "ordinary people" by echoing their demands. In their book *Populism: A Very Short Introduction*, Cristóbal Rovira Kaltwasser and Cas Mudde define populism as an ideology that considers society to be separated into two homogenous and antagonistic groups: "the pure people" and "the corrupt elite," arguing that politics should be an expression of the *volonté générale* (general will) of the people.[8]

The common ground of populist claims is the complaint that the ruling political elites fail to represent the "real" interests of the "real" people. Such claims could be used to discredit perfectly decent regimes, but they could also point to the actual failures of a political system. In most cases, populist criticism embodies a bit of both: a grain of truth enveloped in zealous terminology.

The most interesting definition of populism is offered by the Dutch social scientist Jan-Werner Müller, who describes populism as an "illiberal democratic response to undemocratic liberalism."[9] According to Müller, "populism is seen as a threat but also as a potential corrective for a politics that has somehow become too distant from 'the people.' "[10] Needless to say, concern about the development of a democratic deficit or mounting inequalities has little to do with populism. The mere fact that the masses share a critical view may be disconcerting for the elites, yet it certainly does not make it illegitimate. This is particularly true in an age characterized by liberal elites concerned with their own well-being rather than with their democratic duties.

Liberal elites, Müller argues, are worried about "what they see as illiberal masses falling prey to populism, nationalism, and even outright xenophobia."[11] In one sentence, he adequately captures the patronizing ways in which the masses are perceived: an amalgam of individuals who have no personal autonomy, are unable to make decisions, swayed by passing moods, and are falling prey to notoriously dangerous political movements, of which nationalism is but one example. These claims express disrespect for the personal autonomy of one's opponents. People who are wrong should be corrected; people who are swayed should be stopped. The conclusion is clear, populists should not be given the power to change things; hence their claims are stripped of corrective powers. The accusation of populism is used to restructure the perception of the debate, transform it into a conflict between the rational and the ridiculous, the open and the racist mind, a conflict that calls for victory rather than for a compromise that would lay the basis of a new social agreement.[12]

Nationalism could indeed be reactionary and populist, but the new nationalism we are witnessing is much more than that—it is an expression of a distinct anti-elitist voice that reflects the widening rift between the people and the privileged few, as well as the anger inspired by the growing inequalities and the emergence of "two nations" where there used to be just one. This anger should not be shelved and repressed; it should be given a voice, considered in an attempt to revise the present world order and make it work for the benefit of the many.

In seeking to build a more decent social and political regime, one that provides all citizens better protection and better life chances, it is important to remember that no institution did it better than the nation-state. International organizations are playing a growing role in a wide range of spheres—they determine educational standards, banking and auditing regulations, medical directives, and trade agreements—yet none is able to replace the state in its most important social and democratic roles: allowing individuals to be self-governing, meeting the political challenge of "no taxation without representation," and developing distributive tools and a social support system for those who need it.

Hence, the nation-state should be our primary unit of analysis, argues the American philosopher Martha Nussbaum, "on account of its pivotal importance in setting life conditions for all on a basis of equal respect, and as the largest unit we know until now that is decently accountable to peoples' voices and capable of expressing their desires to give themselves laws of their own choosing."[13] The Harvard economist Dani Rodrik concurs. The nation-state, he argues, is still the best tool for administrating social and economic issues.[14]

In a hypothetical world, globalism may be the answer, but in our fractured reality the few international agencies that exist did not prove themselves to be more independent and less influenced by the powerful, or more efficient in protecting individuals and their rights, than the nation-state. Assuming our goal is to secure the democratic representation of the people and rebuild political trust, the nation-state, rather than some form of globalism, should be our choice.

5

Nutopia

In what may have been one of the most symbolic moments of the last half of the twentieth century, John Lennon and Yoko Ono declared the establishment of Nutopia, a borderless state anyone can voluntarily join. "Imagine" became Nutopia's semiofficial hymn:

> Imagine there's no countries
> It isn't hard to do
> Nothing to kill or die for
> And no religion too
> Imagine all the people living life in peace . . .
>
> You may say I'm a dreamer
> But I'm not the only one
> I hope someday you'll join us
> And the world will be as one.

If you are over fifty, I am sure you can hum along. Maybe you sang it out loud at a sit-in or a demonstration of the peace movement; Lennon's song plays in the background, while people hold hands and light candles, hoping for an open and peaceful world. The influence of "Imagine" on a whole generation and its perception of an ideal world cannot be overestimated. Yet, like all utopian fantasies, this too was a dangerous one. A borderless world is far from ideal; it can be neither democratic nor just. For a democracy to work, individuals need to form an ongoing union, allowing members to test and trust one another's intentions over a considerable span of time.

Game theory teaches us that multiple games played by the same players increase the probability of playing by the rules. If people can leave the game after a certain round they might be tempted to exploit the maximum benefit from that round, ignoring future risks and benefits. In other words, a social contract that does not last for an unknown period of time induces insecurity and raises the chances of social egoism and unfairness. It also erodes the rationality of transgenerational commitments, as the children of those who now invest in structuring some institution or another will grow up, be educated, mature, and age in another social context.

Moreover, when individuals move freely and frequently in and out of a democratic system, it will become unclear who is entitled to vote and who is entitled to be elected. As those who chose the present leadership may have already moved on and newcomers have different and unpredictable interests, whose interests should the elected representatives defend? Who is entitled to make pledges for the future and fulfill political promises? And who should make decisions regarding membership, those who are already members or those who would like to be members?

While writing "Imagine," Lennon aspired to get an American visa; for him the idea that his request could be rejected was inconceivable. Like other members of the elite who have the means to move from one place to another, he believed he had the right to travel freely around the world and live wherever he chose. Indeed, Nutopia is an attractive vision for those who do not depend on the existence of a social network for either their security or their livelihood. In his song "The Other Side of the

Summer" Elvis Costello captured the class bias of the "Imagine" dream, asking sarcastically: "Was it a millionaire who said: imagine no possessions?" Castello was right! The "Imagine" vision served a certain class better than others, and it was these beneficiaries who promoted it as a universal vision.

For globalists, borders are an unnecessary interruption, a hurdle blocking the free flow of capital, skills, and wealth. Hence, they preach free trade and open borders, but the concept of an "open border" is an oxymoron; borders are meant to be closed, to draw a distinction between what is in and what is out; crossing the border must be the exception and not the rule.

Borders are by no means a nationalist idea. No social contract and no system of distribution can function as an open political framework. This is especially true in a democracy. The legitimacy of kings and tyrants does not derive from the boundaries of the exact territory they govern or the population found under their sovereignty. The legitimacy of a democratic regime depends on the support it gathers among its citizens. The question of who is a member thus gains special importance.

Empires moved people around: send them to exile or bring them back home. The will of the ruler and his interests were good enough reasons to include or exclude individuals from a political unit. In a democracy the people choose their leader; the concept of "the people" must therefore precede that of the sovereign. Granting sovereignty to the people and recognizing members of the various social strata as political equals are basic tenets of both nationalism and democracy.

Unlike other identities, nationalism "connects a group of people to a particular geographical place. . . . It is this territorial element that has forged the connection between nations and states, since as we have already noted a state is precisely a body that claims legitimate authority over a geographical area."[1] This sense of connectedness turns a place into a home, and this homely feeling makes people care about the state and wish to participate in its making. Democratic activism is geographically situated—as virtuous individuals we can join others in a struggle to defend their democracy—but it is our democracy that we have an obligation to shape.

Democracy was thus

> born with the sense of nationality, the two are inherently linked, and neither can be fully understood apart from this connection. Nationalism was the form in which democracy appeared in the world, contained in the idea of the nation as a butterfly in a cocoon.[2]

In order for citizens to participate in the democratic process, they must show interest, act, and assume responsibility. The likelihood that they will do so depends on their ability to see the political framework as their own. Only then can social trust be created and a motivation for long-term investments kindled.

Here again, there is nothing specifically nationalistic in this way of thinking; political institutions crave to form long-term political bonding, and for that matter they must create a community that is neither momentary nor meaningless. Open borders and unrestricted immigration are therefore a democratic challenge as much as they are a national one. The major difference between the liberal-democratic and the national conceptions of bordered political communities lies in the ethos of their formation. While liberal conceptions of membership are grounded in voluntarism, national conceptions of membership rely on history and fate. Individuals are assumed to be born into a nation rather than choose to belong to it. This is not a minor difference. Yet, true voluntarism is enjoyed by only a fortunate few. The thousands of refugees who sail the seas in wobbly boats fleeing their demolished homelands and searching for shelter

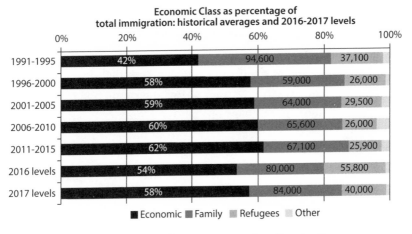

**Economic Class as percentage of
total immigration: historical averages and 2016-2017 levels**

	Economic	Family	Refugees	Other
1991-1995	42%	94,600		37,100
1996-2000	58%	59,000		26,000
2001-2005	59%	64,000		29,500
2006-2010	60%	65,600		26,000
2011-2015	62%	67,100		25,900
2016 levels	54%	80,000		55,800
2017 levels	58%	84,000		40,000

FIGURE 1. Economic class as percentage of total immigration.

soon find out that free movement is not for everyone. The movers who are welcome in the new homeland are mostly those who can, due to exceptional talent or wealth, choose to leave their place of birth and make a new one their home. Even liberal states like Canada and Australia choose their immigrants to fit their needs.

A brief look at Figure 1 will make things clearer. In Canada, one of the most liberal countries from the point of view of immigration policy, more than 50 percent of those allowed to enter have required skills or enough wealth to be seen as productive additions to the social structure, and less than 20 percent (about 60,000 out of 300,000 immigrants, less than 1 percent of the Canadian population) are refugees.[3]

In fact, movement across borders, as such, is much less common than we think. Only 3.3 percent of the world's population lives outside their country of birth. It is therefore fair to conclude that political reality (even in the most liberal of states) does not encourage or allow open movement. In reality, conceptions of membership lean much more in the direction of destiny than choice.

Immigration policies, even generous ones, do not offer principles of demarcation; they take closure as a given and determine a set of exceptions to the rule, nor do they challenge existing borders or the rights of members to determine membership rights; on the contrary, they are grounded in the right of political entities to determine who and how many can join in. Refuges and asylum seekers are an exception to the rule. In such cases the obligation to save lives and prevent harm overrides the right of members to determine the nature of their communion. Yet even in these cases, defining the rules, determining who is to be considered as a refugee, is the prerogative of members.

How can such a decision be made, by whom? What are the principles that would make it fair, and when would it be unacceptable? The scope of this text does not allow me to dwell on these important questions but only to argue that all solutions presuppose closure and some restricted degree of free movement—hence no society is a voluntary association of people gathering together out of their own free will. The liberal and the national ways of thinking converge in real life.

Closure would have been morally and politically less troubling if political units were constructed in a logical way, their borders drawn on the basis of some democratic practice or principles of justice. Unfortunately, no such principle has been found. Questions of demarcation have no democratic answer; one could indeed vote or hold a referendum, yet the outcomes depend on the identity of those who answer the question (as well as on the phrasing of the question itself); we are then caught in a vicious circle.

For example, a referendum regarding the political future of Catalonia will have a different result if it allows the participation of all Spanish citizens or only the Catalonians. As the group defines the result as much as the result defines the group, the legitimacy question cannot find a proper answer in procedure alone. This is where nationalism comes into play, endowing the random process of border drawing with a purpose, providing reasons for its ongoing existence.

Historically, borders were determined in different ways. In a few cases national borders are natural ones; in most instances they are a result of wars and conquests, purchases, marriages, and treaties. All of these processes are less acceptable as a basis of legitimacy in modern times. It is difficult to imagine that in the twenty-first century one could sell or hand over a country as alimony. Excluding such procedures, democratic states must seek legitimacy in national self-determination and self-rule. We are then back to square one, searching for a proper definition of a political self or a nation.

The state and the nation chose each other as partners because: "In the long freedom wars liberalism has won a thousand important battles, securing first the individual and his rights, and then the right of others long excluded from liberty's fruits. But the costs of victory are now being paid: the price of liberal reliance on contract and consent has been the impoverishment of its politics."[4] Negative procedural politics can provide guidelines for fair political action, yet these politics can neither sketch the boundaries of a political entity nor endow a political system with meaning. Nationalism fulfills these tasks in a modern, secular manner. As we shall see, it is a flexible and permissive provider adjusting itself to the needs of the people as well as to those of the state. Nationalism endows the state with intimate feelings linking the past, the present, and the future. The fact that individuals feel they are part of a continuous entity induces in them mutual dependencies and responsibilities and invigorates the will to jointly pursue common ends. Consequently, individuals are likely to develop an entire network of reciprocal attachments, expectations, and obligations. When such a sense of belonging is associated with the state, political institutions turn from bureaucratic entities into an extended family, although the kinship ties in question are highly metaphorical, and though the state is a contingent historical product, it "feels like part of the order of nature; it links individual and community, past and present; it gives to cold, impersonal structures an aura of warm, intimate togetherness."[5]

With the help of nationalism, states turn into homelands— places one is affiliated with due to love and fate rather than due to instrumental considerations. The traditional marriage vows exchanged before building a private home, promising eternity rather than probability, reflect the kind of dedication states would like their citizens to develop: "From this day forward, for better, for worse, for richer, for poorer, in sickness and in health, till death do us part." No patriot could have phrased it more accurately.

Part II

Love and Marriage:

The Virtues of Nationalism

One does not fall in love with a woman or enter the womb of a church, as a result of logical persuasion. Reason may defend an act of faith—but only after the act has been committed, and the man committed to the act. . . . A faith is not acquired; it grows like a tree. Its crown points to the sky; its roots grow downwards into the past and are nourished by the dark sap of the ancestral humus.

ARTHUR KOESTLER, *THE GOD THAT FAILED*

6

Living beyond Our
Psychological Means

Nationalism entered the modern world through a democratic door and an economic corridor, bringing with it a generous alimony: a bottom-up justification for the formation of the modern nation-state. The voyage from Nutopia to the real world suggests that borderless states are dystopian; in order to be democratic and promote justice, states must depend on a clear definition of territory and membership. The need for borders and demarcation is grounded not only in statism, it also touches a very personal chord. In an ever-changing world it helps individuals define their identity, providing them with interpretive tools to decipher reality and make sense of their daily actions.

Categorization is deeply grounded in human psychology—it is a necessary tool of self-definition. The term *human* is a far too thin mode of delineation. Individuals need to rely on "thick identities" to make their lives meaningful. It is therefore appropriate to repeat today, more than two hundred years after they were written, the iconic words of the French intellectual Joseph de Maistre: "I have seen, in my times, Frenchmen, Italian, and Russians. I even know due to Montesquieu, that one may be a Persian; but as for Man I have never met in my life; if he exists, it is without my knowledge."[1]

This is not to say that there are no common human features; we have more in common with members of our species (as well as with other species) than we care to admit. Our individuality, which makes us unique, is formed through a series of exchanges. The features of modern individualism cannot be developed in solitude. Asked to choose an animal he identifies with, Isaiah Berlin said: "A penguin, because penguins live in colonies, they cannot survive on their own." This was his way of saying something profound about himself and about humanity. Humans may be able to survive on their own, yet even the loneliest of literary figures, Robinson Crusoe, had to find Friday to converse with and share the knowledge he had acquired back home—without the ability to converse he would have lost a significant part of his humanity.

It may be assumed that personal autonomy is dependent on our ability to free ourselves from the shackles of belonging, yet freedom is hollow outside of a meaning-providing system.[2] For our choices to be valuable they must have a cultural and normative context. Many of our most personal decisions—the life plan we make, the career we embark on, the family we raise (or choose not to raise)—reflect social, cultural, and religious norms. Modern individuals who wish to shape their life autonomously must first internalize a set of norms and behaviors that would guide their action. The challenge then is to develop social interactions that enrich and liberate the self rather than impoverish and restrain it.[3]

Like morality, identity is a sphere in which no one can be passive. In every choice one makes one must decide whether to be "a contributing partner" or a "free rider"; the former acts within a cultural framework and contributes to its ability to grow and flourish, and the latter flirts with different options other individuals shape, enjoying their efforts to keep such options viable. Identity thus carries not only the mark of our ancestors and contemporaries but also of our own (free) choices. Freedom and determinism keep interacting in our lives, making us who we are.

We define our identity against the background of those things that matter to us. Cultural membership is "the context within which we choose our ends, and come to see their value, and this is a precondition . . . of the sense that one's ends are worth pursuing."[4] Our social and cultural context provides the contours within which choice becomes essential rather than arbitrary, thus transforming freedom into autonomy. Hence, "to bracket out history, nature, society, demands of solidarity, everything but what I find in myself, would be to eliminate all candidates for what matters."[5]

The need to belong to a cultural community, then, is not merely an expression of a psychological craving to live in a known environment and be part of a community to which we can develop feelings of attachment. It is an epistemological need for systems of interpretation that will allow us to understand the world and choose a way of life as well as a creative need for means of interpretation, exchange, and expression.

Like many other goods the importance of feeling at ease with one's identity is highlighted by its absence. Living in a community that supports our identity, we may not be aware of the importance of what it offers, but when we find ourselves in an alien environment, forced to deny or disguise our identity, we experience pain and anxiety. In a beautiful, poetic paragraph Berlin described the state of mind of those individuals who reject their identity and are forced to set out in search of a new one. They are, he writes:

betwixt and between, unmoored from one bank without reaching the other, tantalized but incapable of yielding, complicated, somewhat tormented figures . . . liable to waves of self-pity, aggressive arrogance, exaggerated pride in those very attributes which divided them from their fellows; with alternating bouts of self-contempt and self-hatred, feeling themselves to be objects of scorn or antipathy to those very members of the society by whom they most wish to be recognized and respected . . . it is a well-known neurosis in an age of nationalism in which self-identification with a dominant group becomes supremely important, but, for some individuals, abnormally difficult.[6]

This is why individuals desire to secure for themselves not only a set of Millian liberties but also recognition as members of particular groups and affirmation of the uniqueness and worthiness of such groups. Most of all they demand:

recognition (of their class or nation, or color or race) as an independent source of human activity, as an entity with a will of its own, intending to act in accordance with it (whether it is good or legitimate or not), and not to be ruled, educated, guided, with however light a hand, as being not quite fully human and therefore not quite fully free.[7]

At the heart of modern politics, Berlin concluded, lies "a great cry for recognition on the part of both individuals and groups and in our own day, of professions and classes, nations and races."[8] Not only do individuals see their personal freedom as dependent on their group's ability to be self-governing, they also see their own self-esteem as closely linked to that of their group. Consequently, they regard offenses and humiliations of their group as a personal injury and take pride and satisfaction in the group's success and prosperity.

A significant aspect of maintaining a positive self-esteem is making comparisons that favor the in-group over the out-group. Identity biases perceptions; members of the in-group are seen as bearers of positive values and qualities while members of the out-group are seen as carriers of negative ones. Group membership also biases memory so that "the good actions of the in-group are better-remembered than the bad, and for the out-group, the bad are better-remembered than the good."[9] As positive self-esteem is dependent on an appraisal of both the in-group and the out-group, it is impossible to separate the costs and benefits of membership. A large number of studies led Dominic Abrams and Michael Hogg to formulate "the self-esteem hypothesis" according to which "inter-group discrimination is believed to be at least partly motivated by the individual's desire to achieve and maintain positive self-esteem."[10]

Many have hoped that the need to belong to a nation, or any other particular group, is an expression of a transient developmental stage humanity will grow out of. That group membership will be replaced with a global one, thus abolishing particularism, ethnocentrism, group favoritism, and stereotyping, preparing the ground for global coexistence.

In the wake of World War I, traumatized by the experiences of the war and the loss of young lives, leading intellectuals entertained the idea of cosmopolitanism. Influenced by Kant's "Perpetual Peace" and the moral teaching of the Enlightenment, they were seeking a rational formula that would allow them to establish a human brotherhood that would end all wars. Albert Einstein was among these intellectuals; in his reflections on the causes of war he approached Sigmund Freud and asked him to explain why war persists. Freud's answer expresses skepticism about the healing power of rationality. The ideal condition of things, he wrote, would be a community of men who had subordinated their instinctual life to the dictatorship of reason. Nothing else could unite men so completely and so tenaciously, even if there were no emotional ties between them. But in all probability this is a Utopian expectation.[11]

Compelling individuals to act continually in accordance with axioms that contradict their instinctual inclinations, he concludes, is asking them "to live, psychologically speaking, beyond their means."[12] The great American statesman James Madison was therefore right when stating that "the latent causes of fraction are sown in the nature of Man."[13]

Some, like Kenneth Minogue, argue that nationalism is to be understood "as distortions of reality which allow men to cope with situations which they might otherwise find unbearable."[14] Minogue is right; we embrace ideologies because they make our life bearable and because other options have far more damaging consequences. As the argument will evolve, it will become clear why, despite being fabricated, nationalism helps individuals to cope with the modern world, living active and meaningful lives.

If the behavioral and attitudinal trends cosmopolitans would like to eliminate are deeply inherited in human nature and not the outcome of nationalism, and if they evolve in response to a set of basic needs as old as humanity itself, then it is quite safe to predict that if nationalism were to sink into oblivion, other groups would be formed, allowing people to enjoy a sense of belonging and placing particular affiliations in conflict with universal ones. Humanity has always been divided into communities marked by one set of features or another: families, villages, tribes, localities, nations, states as well as religions, races, ethnicities, genders, classes, and ideologies. Which of these communities has a more negative effect on human behavior?

History tells us that people are ready to kill and die in the name of all of these groups. In recent centuries nationalism has played a major role in evoking hateful and belligerent attitudes, yet such actions could be evoked by each and every one of the abovementioned groups; from Helen of Troy to Romeo and Juliet we have ample proof that even love, the most noble feeling of all, can turn deadly. If subordinating human judgments to pure reason is beyond human means, learning to weigh the dictate of reason against the emotional and moral bias grounded in membership must be our educational and political target.

Social psychology teaches us that membership in a group necessarily leads individuals to express in-group favoritism, but actual dislike or hostility toward the out-group is closely related to the feeling of being subject to "an imposed, unjust distribution of resources."[15] Felt injustice or perceived unfair treatment is a central organizing concept in discussions of intergroup conflict:

> Existing theory and research in social psychology suggests that judgments of injustice provide the cognitive structure and dynamic motivational force that justifies conflictual inter-group behavior.... Perception of injustice of the actions of the out-group lead to protest, retaliation, aggression, and an increase in prejudice. In general, violation of expectations of how rewards should be handed out or how decisions are made (or conflict handled) are the main determinants of inter-group conflict.[16]

Felt injustice raises hostility and violence even among artificial groups. The Robbers Cave experiment is one such well-known example. Muzafer Sherif brought to a summer camp in Oklahoma two groups of eleven-year-old boys and managed to experimentally create felt injustice that led to hostile action spinning almost out of control.[17] These findings are replicated in real life: hostility is therefore more closely associated with felt injustice and a sense of undeserved and biased attitude than the mere fact of membership.

The fact that felt injustice encourages hostility has very little to do with group psychology and is known to us from the dawn of humanity, which was then made up of only four humans: Adam, Eve, and their two sons Cain and Abel. Cain was a tiller of the ground and Abel a keeper of sheep.

> And in the process of time it came to pass, that Cain brought of the fruit of the ground an offering to the Lord. And Abel, he also brought of the firstlings of his flock and of the fat parts thereof. And the Lord had respect to Abel and to his offering: but to Cain and his offering he had no respect. And Cain was very angry, and his face fell. . . . And Cain talked with Abel, his brother: and it came to pass, when they were in the field, that Cain rose up against Abel his brother, and slew him. . . . And the Lord set a mark upon Cain, lest any finding him should smite him.

All the elements of present-day social drama can be found in this first human confrontation: envious comparison, jealousy, hatred, hurt pride, revenge, and violence. The difference between the rival parties was minor and they knew each other well. A deep sense of injustice and wounded pride were all that was needed to spur the first murder. Humanity bears Cain's mark; individuals cannot be envy-free, neither can they ignore the anger invoked by injustice.

Felt injustice is a subjective matter, as members often think of themselves as better, more deserving, than others—even an egalitarian distribution of resources may seem, to some, an expression of injustice. For these reasons, the well-known social psychologist Roger Brown claims that intergroup conflict is "a sturdy three-legged stool. It is sturdy because two legs are universal, ineradicable psychological processes, ethnocentrism and stereotyping; the third leg is a state of society, unfair distribution of resources, which has always existed everywhere."[18] The lesson is clear, in order to reduce social tensions we should spend less time waging a war against the human tendency to gather in groups, and the inevitable outcomes of this tendency—stereotyping, in-group favoritism, and ethnocentrism—and more on joining forces to combat social inequality and injustice.

It is injustice then that we should be dealing with. Preventing the slide of group-oriented attitudes into belligerency requires, above all, a search for decent political agreements. Liberals who aspire to advance peace and reconciliation may be using the wrong kind of social and political tools. They should perhaps care less about reducing the effects of membership in particular groups and more about fairness; in other words, they should develop ways of abolishing social, political, and economic inequalities rather than borders.

Justice will be the main topic of the last section of this book, but a journey exploring the nature of nationalism cannot overlook the inspirational aspects of nationalism that turned it into a powerful motivational tool. Natural selection works in the ideological field as much as in nature. Ideologies survive if, and only if, they fulfill some basic functional needs. The persistence of nationalism proves its effectiveness.

7

Nation Building

Psychology does not mark nations as having any advantages over other human associations; families, tribes, friendships, and unions can also play a mediating role. So what makes nations so powerful and special? In answering this question, two reasons come to mind: one obvious the other unexpected. The former is institutional and relates to the alliance between the nation and the state. No entity is more able than the state to promote ideas in the public sphere. States have collaborated in the past with monarchs, emperors, churches, and political parties, and yet, as we shall see in the following chapters, their partnership with the nation had some exceptionally valuable qualities.

The unexpected, more surprising, reason concerns the fact that the very same features that make nations attractive allies of the modern state—namely, being natural, historical, and continuous entities—are mostly fabricated. In order to establish authenticity and gain the loyalty of their members, nations must therefore continuously be made and remade. This constant creative effort turns nationalism into the most active and engaging social force of the last two centuries.

In its prime, in the heydays of the nation-state, nationalism was an all-encompassing power that shaped both the public and the private sphere. It molded the lives of individuals and structured the fate of whole societies. One must comprehend the uniqueness of this interaction in order to understand the depth of the void created by its absence. This part of the book thus explores the way nationalism shaped the modern state and provided it with tools necessary to turn from an administrative service into a caring entity that takes on itself not merely the role of a neutral coordinator but also that of a compassionate and attentive mother(land).

The caring state defined its duty in paternalistic terms; it did not recoil from educating, guiding, even manipulating the knowledge and feelings of its members. This has allowed the nation-state to form the social solidarity necessary for the establishment of a welfare state, fostering mutual obligations that cross classes, genders, and generations. The fading away of national attachments and the spread of neoliberal views led the state to withdraw from its social and economic involvement, weakening its ideological hold over individual citizens and losing its integrative powers; the lean state became the order of the day. The last part of the book will examine the social and political outcomes of this process and will ponder whether some of the advantages of the nation-state could be recovered.

Throughout the book I argue that the malaise of our age, call it alienation, individualism, the Me decade, loneliness, "bawling alone," is a result of the hollowing of the political community and the weakening of the state. The liberal preference for universal values meant that liberalism nurtured a concept of the person as liberated from all particular relationships, memberships, or identities. Anything that could hold stable meaning and connection was scorned—this meant that cultural ties were dismissed, family ties devalued, connections to the past cut off, attempts to define a common good demeaned. As Deneen argues, in the end, we've all been left terribly alone. "That's the heart of it, really. Liberalism is loneliness. The state isn't our sibling; the market won't be our mate."[1]

Hence, liberalism failed where its major competitors—nationalism and religion—succeeded; putting the universal before the particular, liberalism misunderstood the need for specific identities. A poignant expression of this misconception comes from the architectural field. The liberal resentment of the ornamented symbolic style and its preference for a well-ordered frame of mind was echoed in the Bauhaus vision of worker housing in America. Yale- and Harvard-educated architects wanted workers' houses to have "pure beige rooms, stripped, freed, purged of all moldings, cornices and overhangs . . . it should be liberated from all wallpaper, drapes, Wilton rugs with flowers on them, lamps with fringed shades and bases that looked like vases or Greek columns. It would be clean of all doilies, knick-knacks, mantelpieces, headboards, and radiator covers. Radiator coils would be left bare as honest, abstract, sculptural objects."[2] A perfect representation of a universal architecture suitable to the modern family.

Yet the workers didn't share the dream of brute simplicity and universality. "They bought houses with clapboard siding and high-pitched roofs and shingles and gaslight-style front-porch lamps and mailboxes set up on top of lengths of stiffed chain that seems to defy gravity, and all sorts of other unbelievable cute and antiquary touches."[3] This is not because the workers had no aesthetic preferences, but because, like all of us, they wanted their homes to be particular rather than universal. Fulfilling the task of particularization, nationalism is at its best, and this, among other reasons, is why it is back.[4]

Contrary to liberalism, nationalism went the opposite way, highlighting the particular nature of human relationships. Using acts of narration, organizing historical events into a sequence that has internal and external meaning, it told a story that gave the collective existence a meaning. The national story portrayed the nation as a community of fate, whose storyline stretches from a glorious past to an inspiring future. For nationalists, Anthony Smith argues, the nation was always there, part of the natural order of things. The task of the nationalist is simply to remind compatriots of the past so that they can re-create and relive this glory. Nationalists thus play an active and vital role in the construction of their nations,

> not as culinary artists or social engineers, but as political archae-ologists rediscovering and reinterpreting the communal past in order to regenerate the community. Their task is indeed selective—they forget as well as remember the past—but to succeed in their task they must meet certain criteria. Their interpretations must be consonant not only with the ideological demands of nationalism, but also with the scientific evidences. . . . Episodes like the recovery of Hatsor and Masada, of the tomb of Tutankhamun, the legends of the Kalevala, and the ruins of Teotihuacan, have met these criteria and in different ways have come to underpin and define the sense of modern nationality in Israel, Egypt, Finland and Mexico. . . . In this continually renewed two-way relationship between ethnic past and nationalist present lies the secret of the nation's explosive energy and the awful power it exerts over its members.[5]

Being a modern phenomenon, national energy is invested in processes of "fact finding," thus allowing them to rational-ize their beliefs. The following chapters claim that—using the tools of narration, collective consciousness, and shared memories—nationalism allows individuals to expand their self to the collective sphere, thus endowing their life with mean-ing and allowing them to feel as active authors of their lives.[6] The desire to be autonomous, unrecognized in prenational, predemocratic periods when meaning could have been bestowed from above, makes nationalism an important modern agent that can bridge the old and the new, blend the voluntarism with fate, give an assurance of eternity while expanding the scope of freedom, and encourage individuals to be creative, social agents.

The existence of a nation, argues the French intellectual Ernest Renan, is "a daily referendum."[7] In order to survive, a nation needs to make two moves: "One lies in the past, the other in the present. One is the possession in common of a rich legacy of memories; the other is present-day consent, a desire to live together, a will to perpetuate the value of the heritage that one has received in an undivided form."[8] The national work of recruitment, he argues, is never over, neither is the fear of assimilation. Nation building is ongoing and laborious, a daily attempt to convince each and every member that, for him/her, the national choice is the rational choice.

This is no secret, and here is a well-known example: the unification of Italy created a nationless state; this was rightly seen as an unstable political state of affairs. Nation building became an urgent task; the words of the nineteenth-century statesman Massimo d'Azeglio became an emblem: "We have made Italy. Now we have to make Italians." At the time, Italy did not exist as either a political, cultural, or national entity; only 2.5 percent of its population spoke standard Italian, and many saw themselves as affiliated with the neighboring nations. The different regions had distinct linguistic and cultural traditions, even diverse cuisines. Today, 150 years later, Italy has managed to craft a unified identity, but regional identities are thriving and threaten the union by raising separatist demands. If Italy is to remain united it cannot abandon the work of national maintenance.

The need to supply individuals with reasons for membership forces nations to constantly produce and reproduce the national narrative. In the modern nation-state this effort was state sponsored. Using its extraordinary resources, the state supplied the mechanisms needed to cultivate the national narrative and nurture national feelings; it built schools that taught the national language and spread the national culture; it erected and funded national monuments and museums, sponsored national theaters, national orchestras, national broadcasting services; it constructed squares, gardens, and even cemeteries, established national days, national rituals, and national song competitions, all meant to ensure the animated presence of the nation in everyday life. Each of these acts reinforced the other; in the classroom the teacher told a story that was repeated in the museum, in children's books, and on national TV; national heroes were celebrated, children were named after them, and national days were established to sing their praises. So often was the national story repeated that it was taken to be true.

National narratives are meant to have a moral, representing the nation's better qualities. Think for example about the myth of George Washington and the cherry tree. When Washington was six years old, so the story goes, he received a hatchet and damaged his father's cherry tree. His father discovered what he had done and confronted him. Washington confessed: "I cannot tell a lie," he said, "I did cut the tree." Rather than being angry, his father embraced him. His honesty, he said, was worth more than a thousand trees.[9] It makes no difference whether this is a true description of Washington's childhood. What matters is that it rings true and children could read it in school and take it to be their moral guide. In this case, as in many others, the effectiveness of the story is more important than its authenticity.

As argued, the complex interplay between the (openly) fabricated nature of national myths and their enormous political and emotional power is a testimony to the human need, intensified by modernity and secularization, to belong to meaning-providing communities that extend the boundaries of the self. Nationalism thrives on the human desire to enrich one's limited creative capabilities by sharing one's life with others. It makes this possible by making the boundaries of the self permeable, allowing things that happen to others to enter into the private sphere. The formation of "national consciousness " is a telling example. Consciousness is a private matter; it describes "what affects or goes on in one's own mind."[10] The leap to the collective is not at all natural; it is the result of social and educational processes structured to allow the internalization of a set of beliefs, behaviors, norms, and cultural preferences. The result is an overlap of private cognitive spheres that marks the boundaries of the nation.

In this sense nations are mental structures existing in the minds of their members. A nation, Benedict Anderson states, "is imagined because the members of even the smallest nation will never know most of their fellow-members, meet them, or even hear of them, yet in the minds of each lives an image of their community."[11] Self-testimony is therefore the only way to know whether such an overlap has been established. Like a pair of lovers or a group of friends, a nation is the kind of entity whose existence cannot be inferred from some objective external features. The following two examples demonstrate the importance of self-definition. Members of the Palestinian nation share a religion, language, culture, and territory. However, they do not all share all four characteristics; some are Christians, others live in the Diaspora and therefore do not share a language, culture, or territory with their fellow nationals. A Christian Palestinian living in Jerusalem may share no objective features with a Muslim member of the Palestinian Diaspora, but he does share a territory and maybe a language with a neighboring Jew.

Consequently, an external observer would be unable to divide the world into nations and explain why Jews of Ethiopian, Russian, Moroccan, and Israeli origins belong to the same nation while Palestinians, Jordanians, and Egyptian Muslims are members of different nations. Likewise, it will be impossible for such an external observer to understand why northern Italians and southern Swiss belong to different nations.

Collective consciousness allows members to perceive their nation as a whole. Some argue that this is an ability grounded in modern storytelling, one that presents a plot incorporating a variety of individuals and events that do not occupy the same spatial or temporal space. Indeed for Benedict Anderson it was the modern novel that taught readers to follow the interactions between various characters over space and time. Print capitalism allowed the novel, the newspaper, the poster, and other printed texts to be distributed in a cheap and effective way and "created the possibility of a new form of imagined community, which in its basic morphology sets the stage for the modern nation."[12]

The Old and New Testament as well as the Koran fostered a similar kind of imagination much before the modern novel was invented, yet the human relationships they describe are vertical; they tell a story about a leader and his followers. The modern novel describes people like us, speaking our language, and acting in familiar ways. It therefore allows individuals to form an image of a horizontal society in which we could be included. Moreover, religious texts embody universal aspirations and are expected to be relevant to all readers, everywhere, at any given time. The modern novel is localized, written in the vernacular; it happens here and tells a tale about people motivated by human powers. It does not divide the world between believers and infidels but between us and them.

One of the reasons for the contemporary political crisis, marked by inner conflicts and social polarization, is the disintegration of unifying narratives. The combined effect of processes, ranging from respect for diversity embedded in identity politics to postmodernism, reinforced by a growing antipathy to the state as a mega storyteller, made organizing narratives rare and less effective. One of the prime questions of this century is whether such narratives could be revived and what would be their content.

8

National Creativity

I have already argued that democratic states cannot function as transient associations. Neither democracy nor justice can stand the pressures of short-termism, which is a fatal social and political disease. Yet continuity is not merely a political need; from the point of view of the individual it is no less important. Not only does short-termism undermine our ability to develop a rational life plan, it also reflects on the importance of each and every one of our actions.

Being aware of their mortality, individuals would like to believe their deeds will survive them—nationalism offers them an effective tool of transgenerational presence. Placing one's actions within an unending context endows them with additional significance and makes them part of an aggregated whole whose meaning transcends the individual. A poem or a work of art can stand alone, in some exceptional cases it will be appreciated in its own right. But very often, the value of a creative work can be appreciated only by referencing the works of others, shedding light on a particular narrative, being part of a certain national history or an artistic approach. Referencing magnifies the impact of human actions.

While all the nations of Europe are living out a common destiny, each lives it out according to its own distinct experience. This, Milan Kundera explains, is why:

the history of each European art (painting, the novel, music, and so on) seems like a relay race in which the various nations pass the baton from one to the next. Polyphonic music had its beginnings in France, continued its development in Italy, attained incredible complexity in the Netherlands, and reached its fulfillment in Germany, in the works of Bach; the upwelling of the English novel of the eighteenth century is followed by the era of the French novel, then by the Russian novel, then by the Scandinavian, and so on. The dynamism and long life span of the history of the European arts are inconceivable without the existence of all these nations whose diverse experiences constitute an inexhaustible reservoir of inspiration.[1]

Kundera draws a distinction between art produced within the small national context and that produced within the large global setting. He yearns for the development of a *Weltliteratur* (a world literature) that includes works of genius coming from different national backgrounds. But there is much more to national creativity than that which is created by a gifted few. Most creative actions are local, meaningful in a certain time and place. While they may not be monumental, they enrich the lives of those who create and consume them. *Weltliteratur* is the reign of the gifted few; national literature invites many more individuals to express themselves and feel creatively productive.

In the contemporary Hebrew literature there are few luminaries, but there are many more people of talent whose creativity is important to the whole. I cannot imagine the development of a modern Hebrew culture without their contribution, nor can I think of my own intellectual development without their inspiration. Nationalism, or small context creativity, gave their work meaning and in so doing created a wide space for personal expressions. In this sense, as in many others, the national creative sphere is far more open and all-encompassing than the global one.

As argued, national membership not only intensifies the importance of one's doings, it also promises individuals a place in the ongoing chain of being. We find it difficult to accept that our life will end leaving no traces behind. Religious believers find solace in the afterlife, but for modern secular-minded individuals, mortality can be rebutted only by sharing one's life experiences with significant others.

"A man knows that he is mortal, but he takes it for granted that his nation possesses a kind of eternal life."[2] These words sum up the message communicated by nationalism: nations are here to stay; they can therefore transcend the momentary, shifting finite human experience from the sphere of the mundane and the contingent to the realm of the eternal. This notion of continuity is of particular importance in a modern era, when identification with the nation is "the surest way to surmount the finality of death and ensure a measure of personal immortality."[3]

If nationalism claims to hold a key to eternity, nations must profess immortality. On the verge of their almost certain death in battle, King Henry V promised his men a chance to attain glory by entering the national pantheon as his equals. And so says Henry V to his men:

This story shall the good man teach his son
And Crispin Crispian shall ne'er go by,
From this day to the ending of the world,
But we in it shall be remembered;
We few, we happy few, we band of brothers.[4]

No wonder that during the most difficult days of World War II Winston Churchill approached the British people, echoing this promise: "Let us . . . brace ourselves to our duties, and so bear ourselves that, if the British Empire and its Commonwealth last for a thousand years, men will still say, 'This was their finest hour.' "[5] Soon after, with the support of the British government, *Henry V* was made into a film intended to raise the public spirit. It was "dedicated to the 'Commandos and Airborne Troops of Great Britain the spirit of whose ancestors it has been humbly attempted to recapture.' " Laurence Olivier, riding a white horse, delivering the Crispin Crispian speech, became a symbol for British heroic standing. A speech written by a great playwright, played by a gifted actor, shaped the collective consciousness in ways few real events ever did.

In order to be believed and turned into a collective motivational force, national narratives must be personalized. Like collective consciousness, collective memory offers a way of internalizing events. Remembering is an intimate act of bringing back to mind something from one's own past. Collective memory allows us to recall things that have happened to others. Such recollections are different from knowledge; they invite us to feel as if we, ourselves, had participated in the events. One of the major rituals of Passover is remembering the Exodus of the Jews from Egypt. "In each and every generation," the traditional text reads, "a person is obliged to see himself, as if he personally has left Egypt." The notion of "as if" discloses the active nature of collective memory, turning national historical events into unmediated personal experiences.

Collective memory enriches the personal mind (imagine how impoverished our personal memory would have been if it carried only unmediated memories—namely, if we were to remember only things that have happened to us). Moreover, it creates the basis for an ongoing communal dialogue based on shared moments of glory or despair. The collectivization of memory thus turns individuals from cognitive monads whose experiences are limited and dull into cooperative minds who share words, views, images, melodies, scents, and tastes with others. Like other collective notions, collective memory elevates the conventional, letting ordinary people share the exceptional. In this way it allows for an egalitarian consumption of cultural and historical contributions: from each according to his ability, to each according to his needs.

Forgetfulness, memory's greatest cognitive rival, also plays an important role in the life of nations. Deliberate forgetfulness constitutes an important, and perhaps indispensable, feature of nation building. A nation is a group of individuals who cherish and retain their shared history but remember it selectively, ready to forget some of its less pleasant episodes.[6] Here are two examples Benedict Anderson highlights: the American educational system encourages a view of the 1861–65 armed conflict between the Union and the Confederacy as a civil war within one state and not between, "as they briefly were, two sovereign states."[7] Similarly, English-history textbooks intentionally obscure the answer to the disquieting question of what or whom did William the Conqueror conquer:

> The only intelligible modern answer would be "Conqueror of the English," which would turn the old Norman predator into a more successful precursor of Napoleon and Hitler. Hence "the Conqueror" operates . . . to remind one of something which one is immediately obligated to forget. Norman William and Saxon Harold thus meet on the battlefield of Hastings, if not as dancing partners, at least as brothers.[8]

Deliberate forgetfulness and misrepresentation of historical facts constitute an important, and perhaps indispensable, feature of nation building, allowing different groups to develop a sense of brotherhood.

The handmade combination of remembrance and forgetfulness must be handled delicately, tailored to serve the national purpose, offered to the public in a way that will convince individuals to endorse them. Consequently, their makers are endlessly involved in a process of producing proof and in so doing give birth to most of the modern branches of the humanities nurtured by the nation-state as facts providing mechanisms.

Historical research is the most obvious example of all. So engaged was the historian in his national love affair, writes the Israeli historian Shlomo Zand, that he could not distinguish between the state and the nation and, even more problematically, between the nation and time: "Identity, emotions, national structures seem to him eternal and he stretched them to the end of historical time. . . . His spectacles were thick but they inspired shortsightedness."[9]

History is only one example of "the national sciences" recruited to support the national narrative. Archaeology, geography, literature, linguistics, sociology, art, and biology (among other fields of inquiry) were harnessed to the service of the nation. Research in these fields outlined the boundaries of the nation, described its territory, defined its values, celebrated its traditions, and exposed the glory of the past. The historian, alongside the archaeologist, the geographer, the poet, the author, the painter, the architect, the photographer, the composer, and the biologist, carried a national mission and was therefore venerated and generously funded.

The generous investment in the national sciences fostered the production of collective goods that cannot be individually produced or consumed. In order to enjoy them one must encourage a communal dialogue. Kundera summarizes the essence of our need for others to share a life with in order to expand our consciousness, memory, and imagination:

Friendship is indispensable to man for the proper function of his memory. Remembering our past, carrying it with us always, may be the necessary requirement for maintaining, as they say, the wholeness of the self. To ensure that the self doesn't shrink, to see that it holds on to its volume, memories have to be watered like potted flowers, and the watering calls for regular contact with the witnesses of the past, that is to say, with friends. They are our mirror; our memory; we ask nothing of them but that they polish the mirror from time to time so we can look at ourselves in it.[10]

Nationalism waters our memories, interprets our dreams, and does not allow us to shrink into solitude. The obligation to learn, remember, preserve, and respect is articulated in endless impressive ways the world over. Capital cities are crowded with monuments, museums, squares, and boulevards celebrating national events and national heroes. Schoolchildren tour these places in order to learn about the past and get intimate with the national narrative—"with things that have happened where we are now standing." Monumental representations of great moments in the nation's history are erected and people visit them in order to revive the past in their minds. From Arlington to the Arc de Triomphe the landscape of great cities is crowded with national monuments. The universal nature of this phenomenon teaches us that acts of remembering the past, celebrating greatness, being inspired by remarkable people answer a basic personal and collective need. National consciousness and collective memory form a cognitive map that helps us define who we are, where we are, and where we are heading. Without it we are lost. All of us like to hum, "I did it my way," but looking from afar we discover that most of us did it "our way." Without a collective interpretation that gives meaning to our actions we are likely to be misunderstood or simply unnoticed. Meaning-providing frameworks are therefore as essential as freedom itself.

9

This Place We Call Home

Individuals would like fate to endorse their choices (especially when they are not sure that these are the right ones). Think about the way lovers would like to believe that they are "meant for each other"; "a match made in heaven." They know that it isn't true but arbitrariness is far too frightening. Nation-states are no different; they would like their members to believe that they were destined for each other, a quintessential band of brothers whose bonding is special, different from all other similar bonds. Human relationships, in both the personal and the political sphere, need a reason to be cherished, a reason grounded in the particular. If all attachments are important, how will I choose between them? If all partnerships are alike, why would I prefer one over any other—especially when the one I have chosen may seem, at times, less appropriate than others?

The love of humanity is a noble ideal, but real love is always particular; it targets certain individuals and endows them with some special features that make them (for us) unique. Hence, when asked to give an account of our loved ones we commonly refer to their exceptional qualities. As a grandma, I am well acquainted with "grandma-speak." Most grandmas claim their grandchildren are special, and though logically it is impossible that each and every child is exceptional, such statements sound plausible as they describe a person's inner world rather than an external measurable truth. Nationalism operates much the same way; we know that not all nations are exceptional, not all homelands can possibly be the most beautiful of all. However, we feel our nation to be unique. We depict its peculiarity using trivial images that repeat themselves in other national contexts: its skies are blue and open, the mountains high and mighty, the valleys are green, the rivers wide, and the land bountiful. The words of "America the Beautiful" are an excellent example of this national adoration of the land.

> O beautiful for spacious skies,
> For amber waves of grain,
> For purple mountain majesties
> Above the fruited plain!
> America! America!
> God shed His grace on thee
> And crown thy good with brotherhood
> From sea to shining sea!

Old and new nations alike use the very same vocabulary to inspire nationhood. When a new nation is born it borrows these common symbols in order to make itself unique. Eric Hobsbawm recalls that as a child in the 1920s, he was exposed to an attempt to redraw the Austrian political map.

> "German Austria," this curious and short-lived anthem began, "thou magnificent land, we love thee," continuing, as one might expect, with a travelogue or geography lesson following the Alpine streams down the glaciers on the Danube valley and Vienna and concluding with the assertion that this new rump-Austrian was "my homeland (*Mein Heimat-Land*)."[1]

Despite their banality such descriptions bring tears to people's eyes. For a moment they believe that the grass is greener on their side of the fence.

Nothing exemplifies the interplay between the banal and the inspirational nature of home loving better than the "Home Sweet Home!" signs piled up in supermarkets around the world. People who place them in their kitchen or over the fireplace illustrate how the ordinary can turn special and meaningful. I cannot offer an adequate psychological explanation for how we transform the universal and ordinary into something special. I can only assume that the same mechanism that allows us to fall in love, create friendships and partnerships, and favor those we care about also works in the case of nationalism. A similar psychological mechanism that makes us hum popular love songs in our most intimate moments thinking they were written just for us, allows us to be moved to tears when we hear the national hymn or when our national team wins at the Olympics. The seductive power of the term *mine* influences our judgment and sheds a new light on the way we experience things.[2]

The fact that, using the same political, cultural, and psychological tools, other nations, just like we have, come together to create a similar union does not undermine our feelings, nor does it make our national commitments less special. The most striking example of replication seems the least probable one. According to Conor Cruise O'Brien, virtually every Christian nation adopted the image of a chosen people inhabiting a promised land and applied it to itself. O'Brien provides a partial list of such nations—England, France, Germany, Poland, Russia, Spain, Sweden, Switzerland, and the United States—where this theme was taken up by both whites and blacks.[3] The belief of being chosen is not restricted to the Christian world but is shared by the Jewish people as well as by many Islamic nations such as Egypt, Iran, Iraq, and a host of others.

The fact that national discourse is repetitive does not, however, mean that it is redundant; the same tools are being used over and over again to draw boundaries that are very real. "No nation imagines itself coterminous with mankind,"[4] Anderson claims, and all see themselves as having some distinctive features. Hence an ordinary description of nationalism can coexist with the belief that each nation is exceptional.

The national myth of origins, the biblical story of the Tower of Babel, describes a primordial period (or a state of nature) when humanity was united. In their vanity the people tried to challenge the power of God by building a tower reaching up to heaven. In reaction to this attempt God said:

> Behold, the people is one, and they have all one language; and this they begin to do: and now nothing will be withheld from them, which they schemed to do. Come, let us go down, and there confound their language, that they may not understand one another's speech.[5]

God thus scattered human beings across the face of the earth, gave them different languages, and divided them into nations. From that day onward the complex interplay between the particular and universal has remained an innate feature of human life.

From the iterative nature of nationalism neither pluralism nor chauvinism follows. Recognizing the existence of other nations is inherent in nationalism. It is the way in which other nations are described and treated that distinguishes polycentric nationalism, which respects the other and sees each nation as enriching a common civilization, from ethnocentric nationalism, which sees one's own nation as superior to all others and seeks domination.[6] National claims can thus be analyzed using two distinct and incompatible discourses. The first tells a story meaningful only to fellow nationals; the second encompasses the universal dimension and situates the national phenomenon within a general framework; both cohabit together in the national mind.

10

La Vie Quotidian

THE NATIONALISM OF EVERYDAY LIFE

Contrary to common perceptions, nationalism's greatest moments are not on the battlefield, where all great ideas reveal their ugly faces, but in daily matters, where the American, French, or Israeli ways of life act themselves out. Most of national life occurs in the realm of the banal: nationalism molds our culinary preferences; shapes our architecture and decor; orchestrates the soundtrack of our lives; and fashions what we wear, how we talk, and what we dream about.[1] These are such mundane actions that we tend to overlook the fact that they are ideologically driven. Yet ideologies are at their best when their power is invisible, when they seem natural and can be taken for granted. If asked to connect an activity with nationalism, most people would not put gardening at the top of their list. Nevertheless, gardening, the artificial cultivation of plants and flowers, is an interesting example of the way nationalism shapes our everyday life.

Different national cultures cultivate different schools of gardening, hoping the scenery will echo the national character. In Tom Stoppard's play *Arcadia*, Bernard takes a stroll with his friend Henna, exchanging views about English gardening.

HENNA: This is how it looked until, say 1810—smooth, undulating, serpentine—open water, clumps of trees, classical boat-house.

BERNARD: Lovely. The real England.

HENNA: You can stop being silly now, Bernard. English landscape was invented by gardeners who were imitating foreign painters who were evoking classical authors. The whole thing was brought home in the luggage from the grand tour.[2]

Henna is right; there is nothing real about "the real England," which is an invented construct. However, as we have seen, the fact that a perception is fabricated does not make it less significant. The English narrative successfully tied together greenness and holiness. William Blake's poem "Jerusalem" (which served as an uplifting hymn during World War I) ends with the following words:

Bring me my chariot of fire!
I will not cease from mental fight,
Nor shall my sword sleep in my hand,
Till we have built Jerusalem
In England's green and pleasant land.[3]

Green and pleasant land thus turns from an aspiration to a description of the true England. As Henna wittily notes, in a national era even nature is invented.

Here is another flowery example: When I was ten I received a textbook; I can still remember the brown leather cover holding together thin delicate pages filled with beautiful black-and-white illustrations of the local flowers. *Our Country's Flora* was my guide to nature. Little did I realize its total disregard of the fact that biological habitats do not overlap national borders, that plants, wildlife, and climate do not stop at the checkpoint; they are indifferent to issues of sovereignty and do not care whether this or that part of the land was separated or annexed. Reading

Our Country's Flora, one got the impression that Israel was a unique botanic habitat whose flora and fauna were special and whose borders were natural. One day I came across a nature book published by a Palestinian Israeli. It had the same beautiful sketches of the same flowers and trees, and yet the mere fact that it was written in Arabic made it alien. This was a clear expression of the geopolitical reality of two nations sharing a land, each pretending it was its sole owner. My version of *Our Country's Flora* is just one example of many other nature books that turned into national texts.

In order to emphasize their connectedness to nature, nation-states choose national flowers and plants—the Swiss edelweiss, the Canadian maple leaf, the French iris, the Dutch tulip (a flower originating in Istanbul), and the American rose—as well as national birds like the French Gallic rooster, the American bald eagle, and the Finnish whooper swan, which should not be confused with the Danish mute swan. The purpose is clear: creating a bond between the nation and its land. This is our land; it couldn't have been otherwise—it is God's choice, nature's dictate, history's dictum.

Architecture is another means of shaping the public sphere in the nation's image: celebrating the use of local materials and raising an awareness of the particular beauty of traditional construction methods among local workers and artisans, encouraging them to look at "their thatched roofs, their half-timbering and their gables as if they are born directly from the landscape."[4] Interior decorations and furniture complete the picture by using local materials and images reflecting the beauty of the land.

No doubt the most well-known national representation is the national cuisine. From apple pie to tacos, hummus, and spaghetti, national food is believed to reveal the true nature of a people. It is as hot, sharp, refined, or straightforward as the national character, its ingredients are natural, and the preparation is part of a long tradition passed on by our grandmothers. No wonder motherhood and apple pie are so strongly connected. Each and every nation has its "madeleine" that brings back the smell of home and illuminates our lives in moments of crisis.

According to Eric Storm, the nationalization of the domestic sphere that began in the fin de siècle was prompted by the rise of a new cultural trend driven by a small national elite eager to spread the national message. It had a profound impact on a wide range of areas, like domestic architecture, decorative arts, gardening, and cooking.[5] This process, Storm asserts, became more evident during the early decades of the twentieth century when national activists appropriated all kinds of local or social habits for their nationalist project.

Hence, contrary to the assumption that national identity is shaped in times of crisis, I suggest it is born and sustained in the kitchen, the garden, and the nursery.

> It seems that the most common way of fulfilling national obligations is not through self-sacrifice, or by subordinating one's well-being and interests to the welfare of the collective, but rather by participating in a cultural dialogue. The language we teach our children, the bedtime stories we tell them, the lullabies we sing to them, are as good a way of satisfying our national obligations as a declaration of readiness to die for the sake of the nation.[6]

We have now come full circle. Nationalism, I have argued, entered modernity through a democratic and economic corridor. We can now see that it answers not only the needs of the state but also of modern individuals wishing to become authors of their lives. Nationalism enriches their personal and public experience, endowing their deeds with special importance, making them part of a continuous chain of creation. This creative richness could not have been produced without the supportive hand of the state. The ambition of the modern state to transcend voluntarism and functionality and turn into a unique, exceptional, meaningful, and eternal homeland made it nationalism's best ally.

11

Subjects into Citizens

EDUCATING A NATION

When emphasizing efforts invested in nation building and its ongoing maintenance, it is necessary to visit the most effective and constructive tool—the public school. While in premodern times education was the privilege of kings, gentleman, and landlords, in modern democracies everyone is expected to acquire the knowledge and skills necessary for political deliberations.

As the Reformation encouraged the translation of the holy scriptures into the vernacular in order to allow believers to understand what was being read to them, democracy demanded that people read and write in their own language in order to become effective political agents. Once self-rule was granted on the basis of "one man, one vote," it became clear that knowledge must be evenly distributed. The establishment of public education thus became a necessity. States used schools to spread the narrative and the heritage of the nation, teach the national language, and instill attachment to the state and its symbols. Every child facing the American flag at the beginning of every school day and pledging allegiance to the republic for which it stands— "one nation under God, indivisible, with liberty and justice for all"—is partaking in a national ritual of asserting the unity and values of the nation.

In their formative moments, states comprised mainly of immigrants, like the United States and Australia, as well as states formed by joining together different regions, provinces, or ethnic groups, like Italy, France, or Germany, all embarked on an educational journey intended to transform inhabitants into fellow nationals. Education was the melting pot merging individuals into a national whole, claimed James H. Smart, president of the National Education Association (1881):

> The American school-room is the place in which that wonderful change takes place, by which the children of every land and every tongue, of every religious creed and of every political faith, are transformed by subtle assimilating processes, from aliens and strangers, into a sympathetic membership in the greatest and best political organization the world has ever seen.[1]

So important was education for the formation of a functional modern state that it turned from a right into an obligation. For the first time in human history, acquiring personal skills became a duty.

At the end of the nineteenth century liberals were terrified of giving political rights to people who had no political knowledge. The British philosopher John Stuart Mill did not hesitate to argue that knowledge is a precondition to exercising the right to self-rule and suggested a system of "plural voting."

> If every ordinary unskilled laborer had one vote, a skilled laborer, whose occupation requires an exercised mind and knowledge of some of the laws of external nature, ought to have two. A foreman or superintendent of labor, whose occupation requires something more of general culture and some moral as well as intellectual qualities should perhaps have three. A farmer, manufacturer, or trader, who requires a still larger range of ideas and knowledge, and

the power of guiding and attending to a great number of various operations at once, should have three or four. A member of any profession requiring a long, accurate, and systematic mental cultivation—a lawyer, a physician or surgeon, a clergyman of any denomination, a literary man, an artist, a public functionary (or, at all events, a member of every intellectual profession at the threshold of which there is a satisfactory examination test) ought to have six. A graduate of any university, or a person freely elected a member of any learned society, is entitled to at least as many.[2]

However, he added, "if there existed such a thing as national education or a trustworthy system of general examination, education might be tested directly,"[3] then the proposed differentiation would become unnecessary. In order to be able to meet these goals, national education systems were designed to transcend "the narrow particularism of earlier forms of learning. They were to serve the nation as a whole."[4] In their roles as citizens all individuals were alike; the purpose of public education was to emphasize this equality. With the spread of public education, new groups previously excluded from the educational and the political sphere, the poor, women, people of color, were all given the tools necessary to demand and defend their rights.

In the newly emerging United States of America, public education was taken to be the surest form of protection against tyranny, anarchy, factionalism, and the disruption of law and order. By disseminating knowledge, so it was assumed, all citizens would be able to acquire a better understanding of public affairs and be more likely to make reliable decisions. National education was thus seen as a way of preserving the nation's freedom, encouraging political participation, and fostering a sense of brotherhood. In this spirit, George Washington stated: "Knowledge is, in every country, the surest basis of public happiness. One in which the measures of government receive their impression so immediately from the sense of community, as in ours, knowledge is proportionately essential."[5]

As in other spheres of life, democratic and national knowledge were soon to be combined. Schools taught the national language, nurtured, rehearsed, and remembered the national narrative, venerated national heroes, celebrated the nation's exceptionality (leaving out—forgetting—all that could shatter the preferred national image), fostering national consciousness, imprinting children with the national vision.[6] In his autobiographical *Report from the Interior*, the American author Paul Auster describes his school days in the United States of the 1950s:

> In those early days of your childhood, you were taught to believe that everything about America was good. No country could compare to the paradise you lived in, your teachers told you, for this was the land of freedom, the land of opportunity and every little boy could dream of growing up to become president.... Never a word about the poor black people in your father's buildings, of course, and never a word about the boots worn by the soldiers in Korea.... Nothing about the boots—but scarcely a word about the Indians either.[7]

National education shaped the face of modern democracies. It cemented the belief in equal political rights and opened the door for a new social and political reality based not only on the religious assumption that all men were created in God's image and are, therefore, equal, but also on the belief that each adult can (and must) develop those skills that make him/her a free agent whose judgment should be considered. And though traces of the old Millian privileged view can be found in the way elites try to dismiss the judgment of the less educated, no one dares argue that their vote should be less valuable.

Notwithstanding its deficiencies, national education was the greatest success of the nation-state era. Free and inclusive education became the backbone of the democratic life, disseminating valuable skills that were translated into income, social status, and a wide range of new opportunities. Universal education allowed for the creation of social bonds among members of the different groups now all speaking the same language and sharing some core national knowledge. Its inclusive nature sent an important message: "the state serves more than the particularistic interest of the economic and political elites . . . it is built on universal principles of promoting a 'common good.'"[8]

Different nations formed different kinds of educational systems that reflected their own national character. England, which had a pedigree of rights, based its education on the Magna Carta; the United States, whose democratic ethos was defined by the Constitution, placed liberal values at the core of its teaching. French education shaped after the revolution emphasized its values: "*Liberté, Egalité, and Fraternité.*" As early as 1792, a report was written to the Revolutionary Assembly demanding the establishment of a free system of state education. The failure of the government to establish schools for all citizens, argues the author, the Marquis de Condorcet, deprives individuals of their right to develop their natural abilities and to acquire the knowledge required for performing their civic duties, leaving them less qualified to fulfill their political responsibilities.[9] The purpose of education, he stressed, was to train each individual to "direct his own conduct, to enjoy the plenitude of his own rights and to insure the perpetuation of liberty and equality."[10] Isaac Beer, a Jewish merchant who was granted, in 1791, French citizenship, proudly wrote to his fellow Jews: "Thanks to the Supreme Being and to the sovereignty of the nation, we are not only Men and Citizens but Frenchmen! Our fate, and the fate of our posterity, depends solely on the changes we shall effect in our mode of education."[11]

French education had a cultural mission, it meant to allow the creation of many new Frances and was therefore assigned the important mission of "protecting our language, our customs, our ideals, the French and Latin glory, in face of furious competition from other races, all marching along the same routes."[12] German education had its own set of national tasks. In his well-known *Addresses to the German Nation*, the philosopher Johann Fichte declared that only education could save the German people from moral and political degradation, allowing them to take up their place as leaders of the civilized world. National education was to achieve this goal by suppressing trends of egoistic individualism and fostering devoted loyalty and love to the nation.[13] If Germany was to be saved, Fichte argues, it must, through a conscious control of education, "liberate all the potentialities—moral, intellectual, physical, vocational—for national service."[14]

In a similar spirit the French philosopher Jean-Jacques Rousseau advised the emerging Polish nation to focus on the national education of its young:

> At twenty a Pole should be nothing else; he should be a Pole. When he learns to read, he should read of his country; at ten he should know all its products, at twelve he should know its provinces, roads and towns, at fifteen all its history, at sixteen all its laws; there should not be in Poland a noble deed or a famous man that he does not know and love, or that he could not describe on the spot.[15]

Education, he argues, must shape children's minds and direct their tastes and opinions until they are patriotic by inclination, by instinct, and by necessity.

National education was to encompass a person's life, offering tools for political, cultural, and economic engagement and carrying a promise of equality. It turned subjects into citizens, allowing for the development of a set of linguistic and symbolic skills that facilitate communication between fellow nationals, evoking a willingness to work for the benefit of a common good. Moreover, cultural and linguistic consolidation had an economic and political role; as the group of users of a language or a culture grows larger, more and more consumers join the national pool, improving the payoff of each creative endeavor.

In the nation-state, political communications and official matters, as well as economic exchanges and cultural affairs, were all handled in the vernacular. The power of Latin and other languages spoken by the elites was first eroded then eliminated, a process that allowed the simple citizen to be as politically effective as a member of the elite. For the first time in intellectual history the division between high and low culture was erased, replaced by a new national culture whose boundaries overlapped those of the state. Those who acquired the skills necessary to enter the circles of citizenship, the modern workforce, as well as the national cultural and creative sphere, would never look back.

It is striking to think that only 150 years ago the legitimacy of political power was totally detached from the people. The descendants of Queen Victoria and Christian IX (king of Denmark) occupied the thrones of eight different countries: Denmark, Greece, Norway, Germany, Romania, Russia, Spain, and England. Needless to say, their ties with the royal elites of Europe were much stronger than with the subjects of their own countries. The marriage of nationalism and democracy changed the rules of the game. The rulers had to become acquainted with the people, listen to their voices, speak their language, and very often dress and act like them.

In a society of orders, Greenfeld argues, the claim to status or self-respect "was the privilege of the few, a tiny elite placed high above the rest. The lot of the rest was humility and abnegation, which they tried to rationalize and make tolerable in one way or another, and sometimes even mange to enjoy, but could never escape."[16] Nationalism changed this reality, opening new venues for mobilization and new means for acquiring social status.

For those lacking an aristocratic background, who were estranged from high culture and social etiquette, the emergence of a unified national culture and language was one of nationalism's greatest gifts. New entrance routes to nobility were opened up, and entry tickets were gained by achievements in a variety of fields. Pop singers, actors, soccer players, athletes, artists, and designers were awarded with MBEs and OBEs, even knighted in return for their outstanding services to the nation. The ceremony of Queen Elizabeth knighting Sir Paul McCartney captured this moment of change. In this new age of modern nationalism it became conceivable that when she goes to bed, rather than humming some religious hymn in Latin the queen quietly chants to herself: "She loves you yeah, yeah, yeah."

12

A Short History of the Cross-Class Coalition

We have already seen how nationalism erased the difference between high and low culture by creating a unifying language; how national culture cemented social bonds and made people feel closer to one another; how national narratives sealed this partnership by nurturing a set of social and political points of view grounded in a shared national consciousness. We followed the way nationalism created a unifying narrative, understanding the economic implication of such a move. Teaching the national language and spreading a shared culture prepared the ground for the emergence of the modern economy. In traditional agrarian societies, "each occupation could develop its own idiosyncratic culture by which the skills, the 'secrets,' and the ethical codes were transmitted from one generation to another."[1] Diversity of language had not, therefore, caused particular problems; it could even support social stability by providing a clear sign of the position occupied by each and every member.

The close affinity of class, occupation, and language is well illustrated in George Bernard Shaw's classic play, *Pygmalion*. Eliza, the flower girl, comes to Professor Higgins to learn proper English so that she can get a better job: "I want to become a lady in a flower shop stead of selling at the corner of Tottenham Court Road. But they won't take me unless I can talk more genteel."[2]

By the end of the play, Eliza has acquired linguistic skills that define her new identity; she can no longer go back:

> I can't. I could have done it once; but now I can't go back to it. Last night, when I was wandering about, a girl spoke to me; and I tried to get back into the old way with her; but it was no use. You told me that when a child is brought to a foreign country, it picks up the language in a few weeks, and forgets its own. Well, I am a child in your country. I have forgotten my own language, and can speak nothing but yours.[3]

National education made a heroic attempt to erase (or reduce) class differences, thus creating the conditions for internal mobility, opening up for members of the lower classes a wide range of political and economic opportunities. Sharing a language reduced training costs, encouraged people to move from one part of the country to another, and enabled social and economic change. The homogenization of culture and language served both the economic need for professional adaptability and the democratic demand for shared deliberations. Nationalism, democracy, and the (internal) mobility of labor reinforced one another, bringing the classes closer together, allowing discourse across different social groups, making the nation-state the first political entity grounded in a social-cultural alliance that gives place to the people as well as the elites.

Although nationalism started as a project of the elites, in order for it to materialize, the elites had to gather the support of the people. For that purpose, they have created a cross-class coalition offering all citizens a set of valuable goods and opportunities. It is important to emphasize that for social cooperation to prevail, participants need not attain identical goods and benefits; it is sufficient that they secure for themselves significant benefits they could not have otherwise acquired. What were the benefits the nation-state guarantees its members?

Democratic nationalism justified the creation of new political units, thus allowing elites to concur on new grounds. Power was transferred from the monarchs and their courts to the hands of the many; political elites and state bureaucrats assumed the task of fostering the new political institutions; intellectual and creative elites joined forces to fashion the national culture and narrative; financial and industrial elites worked together to produce the nation's wealth; military elites and security forces were recruited to defend the nation; the intellectual elites benefited from nurturing the national sciences, while those who mastered new professions—communication, music, sports, and the arts— were encouraged to perform and create. Members of the different elite classes thus benefited from the shift of power from monarchs and autocrats into the hands of the nation. After seizing power the elites turned to recruit the people to support and protect their project. National movements, Tom Nairn claims, have invariably been

> populist in outlook and sought to introduce lower classes into political life. In its most typical version, nationalism assumed the shape of a restless middle class and intellectual leadership trying to set up and channel popular class energies into support for a new state.[4]

In the days of the French Revolution the middle classes employed the idea of the nation to motivate the people to fight against the old regime that had prevented them from acquiring political rights. In the nineteenth century elites seeking new opportunities employed national justifications to enlist the masses in their struggle for self-rule. In the age of decolonization the intelligentsia collaborated with the middle classes in a struggle against external oppressors in order to secure the political and economic benefits inherent in independence. In their struggle for political power and opportunities, the different classes walked the same route. Although they did not enjoy the same benefits, participation granted each and every member significant paybacks; the most important of these was the acquisition of citizenship, a right now secured to all.

While in previous periods, "possession was the only real source of power, and no distinction was made between economic and political power,"[5] in the age of the nation-state, membership in the nation became the relevant criteria for inclusion (and exclusion). Wealth, education, skills, and social status were still relevant for the distribution of power but could not be used as benchmarks for participation in the political game. This unprecedented state of affairs offered extraordinary benefits to those who had no wealth, education, or status, nor any prospect of acquiring them. "Nationality elevated every member of the community which it made sovereign. It guaranteed status. National identity is, fundamentally, a matter of dignity. It gives people a reason to be proud."[6]

By making them part of a social and collective political unit the nation-state offered members of the lower classes a set of irreplaceable goods: by granting them education, teaching them a common language, and ensuring their political rights, it allowed fellow nationals to experience, within the national sphere, unprecedented freedom.

National solidarity supported the transformation of the nation-state into a welfare state in which individuals enjoy full membership, "not only as bearers of civic rights or as political participants, but as mortals buffered by misfortune and unsettled by insecurity."[7] Society's disinherited members were thus given permission to claim social benefits as well as protection from tangible risks. This was one of nationalism's greatest gifts, allowing the less privileged to profit and to enjoy a set of social goods and social services[8] grounded in rights rather than in generosity or benevolence. Citizens need not beg to be allowed to participate in the political sphere, to be educated, or to receive welfare payments; they are able to demand these goods by virtue of their political standing. Nationalism thus offered the masses the most desirable benefit of all—human dignity. For those who had no pedigree, no property, and no work, nothing could be more valuable. Acquiring the legitimacy to make social or political demands, and realizing these demands are entirely different, matters. Many of the claims for welfare, health, and education were left unmet; nonetheless, there is a world of difference between not receiving a service and not being able to claim it.

Although it didn't abolish the class structure or class differences, the nation-state gave members of all classes a reason to participate in a collective effort to form a national political unit that would benefit (albeit in different ways and to a different extent) all its members. Marxists argued that nationalism was an ideology capitalists used to ensure control over the national markets, "a sort of cultural diversion to hide economic exploitation."[9] Yet they failed to see that even those economically exploited acquired new political powers and social benefits; they were no longer vassals but independent social agents.

The obligation to answer the needs of members of all social classes was not the only reason why the emergence of the modern nation-state overlapped with that of the welfare state. Necessity advanced the development of new systems of distribution; the Great Wars fought by national armies, causing severe damages, scarring the home front as well as the battlefields, sparing neither rich nor poor, paved the way for inclusive social policies. Political leaders were looking to preserve the social unity created by the wars and extend it into better times: "Wartime hardships created a sense of social cohesion and unanimity, and a wish to continue the new spirit of equality into the peace and to temper inherited class divisions."[10] This spirit was reflected in the preamble of the French law of social security legislated soon after the end of World War II (October 1945). The law was meant to preserve "the spirit of brotherhood and reconciliation of classes that marked the end of the war."[11] The feeling of shared national destiny and shared responsibility was translated into distributive social policies offering new entitlements and rewards. The newly created national social services, like national health services and social security, benefited citizens and gave the social contract a new meaning.

Hence, despite social and educational inequalities, it was logical for the less well-off to ally themselves with the national project. Contrary to the Marxist claim, the willingness of the working classes to participate in the formation of nation-states was not motivated by false consciousness but by rational considerations. While Marx understood well the motivating power of capitalists and their urge to create ever-growing markets, he failed to understand the spirit of the workers. The nation-state offered them gains far more valuable than an international class struggle could have ever granted. Thus, to Marx's disappointment, the lower classes embraced nationalism and made it the most popular ideology of the twentieth century. National loyalties and national struggles took precedence over class solidarity. The class war was to be postponed for at least another century.

Part III

A Divided House

It was the best of times, it was the worst of times, it was the age of wisdom, it was the age of foolishness, it was the epoch of belief, it was the epoch of incredulity, it was the season of light, it was the season of darkness, it was the spring of hope, it was the winter of despair.

CHARLES DICKENS, *A TALE OF TWO CITIES*

13

The Breakdown of the Cross-Class Coalition

The spread of globalism alongside the enchantment with "the end of history" enhanced the feeling that the West had entered a steady equilibrium with no enemies to fight and endless economic opportunities to enjoy. The state that was seen as a protector and an enabler in the post-world-wars period turned into a menace that must be restrained. While the fear of despotism and totalitarianism led liberals to restrict state involvement in the public sphere,[1] right-wing ideologists expressed a preference to reduce state bureaucracy and regulatory powers in the name of individual liberties and economic efficiency. Noninterference and nonregulation became the new political and economic buzzwords. This unexpected alliance forced the state, and with it the nation, to withdraw from the public sphere, claiming moral and cultural neutrality and practicing nonintervention. This was the perfect moment for neoliberalism and globalism to take over.

If the liberal state must remain forever a philosophically empty form, argues the French philosopher Jean-Claude Michéa, "what else is there than the Market which can fill the pages it leaves blank, and in the end takes on the task of pronouncing the morals? The political liberalism of Benjamin Constant is not a one-way ticket. It always includes, whether you like it or not, the return to Adam smith."[2] When the idea of laissez-faire settled in as a major guarantor of freedom, privatization, deregulation, and free trade were quick to follow. Poverty replaced class, and charity is substituted with welfare.

With the spread of globalism and neoliberalism, the powers newly acquired by citizens were becoming more and more vacuous and less applicable in everyday life. Globalism depreciated the value of the benefits offered by the nation-state. To begin with, it created a democratic deficit, eroding the influence of citizens over decisions that shape their lives. Those who had just recently entered the political sphere suddenly found out that the state was slowly succumbing to external forces (international or regional organizations, NGOs, and transnational corporations) over which they had little, or no, influence. Consequently, notions such as self-rule or independence became more opaque than ever. Under such circumstances citizens

> constitute less and less of an entity capable of expressing a collective sovereignty; they are mere juridical subjects, holders of rights and subjected to obligations, in an abstract space whose territorial boundaries have been increasingly vague.[3]

The erosion of national citizenship influenced not only the political standing of individuals but also their economic status. The allocation of social and political status on the basis of mere membership that was typical of the national way of thinking gave way to a neoliberal understanding of status grounded in skills and performance. Never had competence been so intensively pursued; those who have the required skills are offered unlimited opportunities, those who don't are left behind. The skills and competencies required for mobility and adaptation are no longer grounded in any particular national feature. National cultures, and especially national languages, are of little use to members of the mobile classes (and may even be an obstacle). If I want my children to enter the global market, their first language should be English (or Mandarin) rather than Hebrew and they should feel more at home wherever their iPhone and computer have easier access to Wi-Fi than in the town where they were born and raised. Rather than their fellow Israelis, their compatriots would be other English speakers, users of social media, fans of globally watched reality shows, megastars and celebrities they follow on Instagram or Facebook, and their peers, graduates of elite schools and Ivy League universities, players in the global market. When the value of national languages and cultures is depreciated, the eagerness to support them declines. Having less of a political and economic motivation to invest in the making and remaking of the nation, the mobile elites shift their interests and resources elsewhere. National ties become relics of the past—sentimental perhaps but of decreasing social and economic value.

National public education is the main victim of globalization. It was the jewel in the national crown, nurturing citizenship skills, opening up new professional opportunities, and easing mobility within the boundaries of the national economy. Established in order to teach the national language, transmit the national heritage, enhance national identity, and strengthen bonds of solidarity among fellow nationals, public (national) education served to consolidate the society and bridge social and economic gaps. Today, it is outdated. In order to prepare children for a global world it must give up some of its most notable achievements.

It is clear why those who favor globalism regard national education as ineffective and opt for private schools they can shape to fit their purposes. Others are also dissatisfied. They had high hopes—education was supposed to be a social game changer, yet once the doors of the classroom were opened to include all members of the society, the newcomers found that schooling could offer neither mobility nor economic success. Now they realize that their children will be better educated yet poorer than their parents. Their frustration is further intensified by the fact that traditional education systems are unable to provide children with the skills necessary to succeed in the global economy. National education thus reveals itself as less of a salvation than anticipated. Fifty years ago, Yvonne Roberts asserts,

> education was the magic word, facilitating social mobility no matter how deprived a child's background. Recent research tells us this is no longer the case. On the contrary, in the unevenness of its delivery, it appears to be the cause of social exile for too many young people.[4]

The inability of national education to play its designated mobilizing and integrative role is one of the main reasons that the state lost the respect of its citizens. This is particularly true since the language of educational equal opportunities kept dominating the political discourse long after it was proven vacuous.[5] The gap between state promises and the ability to fulfill them contributes to the erosion of trust in governments and the ongoing weakening of state apparatus.

Schools are made less relevant not only because of their inability to allow a real meritocracy to develop but also because they are deprived of the role of promoting social cohesion. In the *Closing of the American Mind*, Alan Bloom criticizes modern liberal philosophy for placing self-interest and self-expression at its core. For Bloom, this created a void that was filled by postmodern ideologies celebrating diversity and relativism. The failure of contemporary liberal education, he argues, has led to a sterile social dialogue in which commercial pursuits have become more highly valued than the search for truth or for a common good. Although Bloom's alternative is, I believe, far too conservative, his basic question still resonates: "when there are no shared goals or vision of the public good, is the social contract any longer possible?"[6]

Unable to fulfill its most basic traditional goals—namely, preparing children to cope with future social and economic tasks, supporting social mobility, and nurturing social cohesion—national education became one more divisive force. The crisis did not skip higher education, which also became a source of public disappointment. More people than ever attend higher education institutions, but graduating—especially from an institution that is not one of the few Ivy League institutions— no longer guarantees a suitable job or entry into the ever-shrinking middle class. All over the world, the growing frustration of the educated poor is motivating social and political unrest. With education no longer fulfilling its traditional social and political role, the gratitude associated with getting educated has evaporated; it has turned sour.

Disappointingly, higher education also promotes social polarization, cultural differences, and political schisms: as members of different classes and social groups attend different universities and are being socialized to hold different values and beliefs. Arlie Russell Hochschild compares voluntary activity groups at Louisiana State University and the University of California, Berkeley, both large universities with over 30,000 students. The 375 active student groups found in the former included the Oilfield Christian Fellowship, the Agribusiness Club, and the Society of Petrophysicists and Well Log Analysts. None of these has equivalents at Berkeley with its 1,000 active student groups, among them Amnesty International, the Anti-Trafficking Coalition, and Global Student Embassy.[7] This is just one example of the way in which higher education sharpens social, economic, and cultural gaps.

The collapse of unifying institutions on the one hand and the emergence of new global realities on the other eroded the notion of collective fate essential for the development of a national worldview and with it the readiness to share national and private resources and responsibilities. Sharing resources and social responsibilities is logical for those who anticipate spending a lifetime together; it is far less so for those who expect to move from one political entity to another. As I have already argued, there is a good reason why democratic welfare states are grounded in closure that ensures the persistence of stable and continuous communities, allowing for lifelong and often cross-generational bonds to develop. In a world of permeable borders, where social stability is no longer guaranteed, the "haves" have less reason to share and the "have-nots" are left unprotected.

Old money elites were not more virtuous than their predecessors; however, their scheme of risks and opportunities tied them to their communities in ways that do not apply to the new elites who are permanently "on the way"; if they haven't yet moved they are about to move, come back, or go away again. Those in transit have no interest in fostering social solidarity. The fact that affluence has been dissociated from the ownership of land and real estate has made wealth portable.

The forefather of modern liberalism, John Locke, believed that voting rights should be attached to the ownership of tangible property. While this could be regarded as a way of privileging the rich and the powerful, it emphasizes the link between voting rights and property that grounds one in a community. In his clairvoyant book, *The Revolt of the Elites*, Christopher Lasch describes the way in which the elites have deserted their societies. There were always privileged classes, he argues, but they were never isolated from their surroundings:

In the nineteenth century wealthy families were typically settled, often for several generations, in a given locale. In a nation of wanderers their stability of residence provided a certain continuity. Old families were recognizable as such, especially in the older seaboard cities, only because, resisting the migratory habit, they put down roots. Their insistence on the sanctity of private property was qualified by the principle that property rights were neither absolute nor unconditional. Wealth was understood to carry civic obligations.[8]

Those days are over, and today those who stay at home forfeit the chance for upward mobility: "success has never been so closely associated with mobility."[9]

A study published in 2016 by New World Wealth revealed that the most rapidly growing group of immigrants is the millionaires. Since 2013 the number of "millionaire immigrants" has grown by 60 percent. While they are still, proportionally, a small group, they nonetheless set the tone. The flight of the rich and powerful should worry nations as much, if not more, than the arrival of "the tired and poor"; the former might erode the wealth of a nation, the latter may, if properly handled, help build it.[10]

The new elites, Lasch argues, rebel against those who try to hold them back. They "congregate on the coasts, turning their back on the heartland and cultivating ties with the international market. . . . It is a question whether they think of themselves as American at all."[11] It is regrettable that these words did not echo more loudly in liberal democratic circles, as they could have led to a process of self-reflection and may have even prevented the present state of affairs.

The growing rift between the haves and the have-nots leads them to hold different values, norms, and political beliefs, reflecting their assessment of their life chances. Attitudes toward free trade exemplify this tendency clearly. While the consensus among mainstream economists is that free trade is desirable, there is no such consensus among the voters. An analysis of the views individuals hold on this issue show high correlation with economic status measured in terms of income. "Individuals who rank high in the domestic income distribution or consider themselves to belong to the 'upper classes' are significantly more likely to be pro-trade. It is relative income not absolute income that seems to matter."[12]

As expected, antitrade attitudes and protectionism correlate significantly to neighborhood attachments, nationalism, and patriotism, whereas free-trade attitudes are associated with cosmopolitanism.[13] The same correlation repeats itself in matters regarding the free movement of people. Those who resent free trade are also threatened by immigration. They object to the fact that "national boundaries become totally porous with respect to goods and capital and even more porous with respect to people who are simply viewed as cheap labor—or in some cases cheap human capital."[14] They see immigrants as invaders who enter their national sphere, violating its unity, demanding a share of goods created collectively.[15]

The risk of losing their economic and social status motivates individuals to be suspicious of "others" who might threaten their social position. Weakness and fear inspire calls to erect walls and protect members from newcomers. Realizing that there is no place for them in the global sphere, the immobile wish to use their political power in order to force the mobile to remain within the national framework and pay their dues.

To their dismay, they find that today's elites wish to become nationless; they do not see their success as connected with the future of any specific nation or state. They build their home(s) and stay in them the exact number of days their tax consultant advises. They send their children to the best global schools and universities that can secure their future. They buy and sell commodities in the international stock exchange and own homes in several countries. They ski in the Alps, sunbathe in Bermuda, and enjoy theater in London and restaurants in Paris. In fact, the elites of the world have been united; they are citizens of the world and would not like any national affiliation to be forced on them.

Those less affluent, less educated, and less skillful fear being thrown into the global competition as their chance of winning are minute and the price of failure unbearable. They tend to prefer "a bird in hand than two in the bush." They hope to protect local opportunities by slowing down globalism while making national borders higher and less permeable than ever. They call on their states to protect them, defending them from misplacement and exploitation, helping them to take control over their lives. While searching out ways to secure their future they are likely to cling tightly to their national and religious traditions and seek solace in God and nation.

The workers of the world will never unite. They have no real interest in doing so. Nationalism is, therefore, here to stay, turning from the vision of the elites into their nightmare. The present wave of nationalism is not, as many have suspected, driven by irrational forces; it is a rational response grounded in the self-interest of the masses eager to protect themselves from a global dream they cannot share.

14

One Nation, Divided, under Stress

As has been argued, many assume that the emergence of nations in general and of nation-states in particular was an evolutionary stage that must be transcended. History, it is claimed, develops linearly:

> from the small group to the larger one, from the family to tribe to region, to nation, and in the last instance, to the unified world of the future in which . . . the barriers of nationality which belong to the infancy of the race will melt and dissolve in the sunshine of science and art.[1]

A united humanity may be an attractive vision, yet it is nowhere in sight. States have not been replaced by other types of global political structures; instead, they are carelessly ripped apart in ways that bring about national and international chaos.

One of the biggest threats to states' unity results from the individualist nature of contemporary globalism. In his book *The World Is Flat*, Thomas Friedman defined three stages of globalism:

> while the dynamic force in Globalization 1.0 was countries globalizing and the dynamic force in Globalization 2.0 was companies globalizing, the dynamic force in Globalization 3.0—the force that gives it its unique character—is the newfound power for individuals to collaborate and compete globally. . . . No one anticipated this

convergence. It just happened—right around the year 2000. And when it did, people all over the world started waking up and realizing that they had more power than ever to go global as individuals, they needed more than ever to think of themselves as individuals competing against other individuals all over the planet, and they had more opportunities to work with those other individuals, not just compete with them. As a result, every person now must, and can, ask: Where do I as an individual fit into the global competition and opportunities of the day, and how can I, on my own, collaborate with others globally?[2]

Friedman's description accurately captures the way today's globalism erodes the power of states and encourages competitive individualism. Yet, like many other commentators, Friedman overlooks the conflict-ridden effects of this phenomenon. Mesmerized by the power given to the few to freely enter the global game as equals, he overlooks the social and political price associated with the inability of the many to make the same move.

Friedman's description of globalism makes two vital points. First, it emphasizes the fact that the move to Globalization 2.0 and 3.0 was quick and unintended: reality preceded ideology, things happened, and only then were they understood, justified, and finally theorized. Second, it explains why this process motivated individuals to free themselves from their political and national base in order to improve their competitiveness. In the age of Globalism 3.0 the range of opportunities is endless, yet the ability to take advantage of these opportunities is more limited than ever. The recurrent saying, "in China if you are one in a million, there's still 1,300 just like you," could be rephrased globally: if you are one in a million, there are still 7,500 people just like you, and the numbers keep growing every day.

The globalization of individuals (rather than of states or international organizations) can be seen as providing the highest degree of personal freedom: social institutions lose the power to restrain personal freedom, and the world is leveled in ways that open up new venues for all. It seems as if nothing stands between individuals and their success but human skills and hard work. For most individuals, however, this description is quite untrue. Globalism 2.0 + 3.0 enlarges the gulf between the different classes, eroding nationalism's most powerful tools: a stable cross-class coalition that makes all fellow nationals supportive of one another, partners in generating common goods that otherwise could not have been secured.

The mounting risks of some and the diminishing opportunities of others have created two nations where once there was one. In *The Vanishing Middle Class*, Peter Temin provides a bracing reflection of the two Americas.[3] America, he argues, is now made up of two groups: the "FTE sector"—the people who work in finance, technology, and electronics—and "the low-wage sector." The FTE citizens rarely visit the country of the low-wage sector, where the world of possibilities is shrinking, often dramatically, and where people are burdened with debt and anxious about their insecure jobs, if they even hold one.

> Many of them are getting sicker and dying younger than they used to. They get around by crumbling public transport and cars they have trouble paying for. Family life is uncertain here; people often don't partner for the long-term even when they have children. If they go to college, they finance it by going heavily into debt. They are not thinking about the future; they are focused on surviving the present. The world in which they reside is very different from the one they were taught to believe in. While members of the first country act, these people are acted upon.[4]

Members of the two nations rarely meet, live nearby one another, have a serious conversation, or befriend each other. Following the 2016 elections, the *New York Times* described an America divided into "the Clinton nation" and "the Trump nation," each belonging to a different social and economic class. America is not alone.[5] Right after the Brexit vote many commentators in Britain described a country divided into "two nations which are staring at each other across a political chasm."[6] Similar comments were made in Israel, France, Spain, Turkey, Germany, and more, reflecting the enormous changes that separate nations into different social classes that do not share a common fate.

As the following maps demonstrate, election results in different countries give this phenomenon a visual expression: two nations geographically divided, culturally dissimilar, economically disjointed, and politically opposed. The mega cities and shores constitute islands of progressive liberal democratic voters set in a vast right-wing, nationalist, and conservative ocean. The coastal periphery looks beyond state boundaries and wants to be emancipated; the heartland, the home of what has been termed the new reactionary class, looks around in anger and frustration and wants to be saved. In this sense countries as different as Turkey and the United States are very similar.

One of the most interesting lessons to emerge from these maps is that in the age of Globalization 2.0 and 3.0, class differences allow us to predict individual behavior more than national affiliations. As social crisis moves in, moving out of a poverty-stricken neighborhood or town to a more affluent one is harder than emigrating. The result is social and economic stagnation. "The probability of ending where you start has gone up, and the probability of moving up from where you start has gone down."[7] Reaching the top ranks is tougher as the rungs of the social ladder have grown further apart. To borrow an overused feminist

FIGURE 2. The Turkish referendum map, 2017.

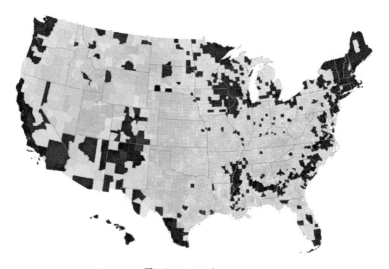

FIGURE 3. The American elections map, 2016.

idiom, it seems as if the rich and the poor inhabit two different planets.

Class divisions are no longer simply a matter of ownership over the means of production. The complexity of markets makes exploitation harder to define, and the relationships between the input of a worker's labor and the value of a product quite impossible to trace. Rather than being grounded merely in the distribution of means of production or wealth, the new definition of class reflects the scheme of risks and opportunities individuals face.[8] Individuals belong to the same class if they share a similar set of opportunities and risks and a related cluster of hopes and fears that influence their evaluation of their life chances. This evaluation directs them to endorse certain social, political, and economic policies that will minimize their risks and expand their opportunities.

Consequently, poor and rich across the globe endorse political perceptions that reflect their economic positions and place themselves at different points along the Global (G)–National (N) continuum. For the few who can make it, the move to Globalization 2.0 and 3.0 is emancipating; for the many who are less capable of competing in the global marketplace, it induces helplessness and nihilism. To the disappointment of many, class, rather than norms, values, or levels of moral development, differentiate globalists from nationalists.

15

The Elephant in the Room

Although the breakdown of social cohesion did not escape public attention, the magnitude of the phenomenon went unnoticed. Data show that in the 1980s, just when liberals were celebrating their ideological victory, social and economic gaps started building up. It took over twenty years for the process to be seen not as a coincidence but as a major social and economic change. Even then, its profound consequences remained unclear.

In her eye-opening book *Living in Denial*, Kari Marie Norgaard tells a local story with a universal message. The story is located in Bygdaby, a small Norwegian town that has experienced the brutal outcomes of climate change. Norgaard discovered that for the highly educated and politically savvy residents of the town, global warming is both common knowledge and unimaginable at the same time; every year there is an "exceptionally warm winter," and they keep waiting for it to be colder the following year. Norgaard carefully traces the development of socially organized ways of thinking that allow individuals to collectively distance themselves from information that threatens their worldview. Understanding the links among denial, cognitive dissonance, and privilege, she argues, "affords us another important view through the kaleidoscope. Situating cognitive dissonance and denial in the context of privilege underscores the relationships among individual emotions, culture and social structure."[1]

Like the residents of Bygdaby, the liberal progressive elites of the West knew that something was going terribly wrong: social and economic gaps were growing rapidly, unprecedented wealth was being concentrated in the hands of a few, social mobility was slowing down, and social trust was eroded. As a result of automatization, globalization, and free trade, many honest working people found out that they could not make a decent living. Last but not least, demographic changes were creating new political and social realities that were raising social discontent. More and more people were starting to feel insecure about their futures. In the national age social changes were mediated, presented as a means of achieving widely accepted shared goals. In the postnational period changes happened and individuals were left to deal with their consequences on their own. Like other social changes, Globalization 2.0 and 3.0 were unplanned and their outcomes unintended. Liberalism's initial intention was to secure justice and liberty for all, but in seeing freedom through an economic prism, giving priority to the free market over other kinds of freedom, liberalism lost its balance.

In this process globalism turned from an instrument of the state to its rival. It is now difficult to remember that in its early days, globalism was seen as another tool of colonialism—a way of allowing the developed world to exploit the developing world without bearing the costs of conquest and domination. The elites of the West believed that globalization would turn the world into their playground, allowing them to invent and invest using the whole world as the sphere of their entrepreneurship. They envisioned bringing together human capital trained in one continent, financial capital accumulated in another, and cheap labor inhabiting a third in order to develop new economic opportunities. The global free market was supposed to allow them to enjoy the fruits of their skills and resources regardless of national borders or civic affiliations. Indeed, workers in the developed world were losing their jobs, and major industries were transferred to the East, but there was an influx of cheap commodities and new occupational opportunities that seemed to compensate for the loss of other, less attractive, jobs. Some social thinkers did warn that globalism would hit "working people in the United States who may be losing their jobs, farmers maneuvered off their land, city dwellers who may have to accommodate waves of landless immigrants."[2] Yet the loss was expected to be compensated by excessive consumerism. Even when you earned less, you could still have much more, and the commodities you purchased would make you feel richer than ever.

In the developed world in general and the United States in particular people believed that they would permanently be on the winning side of globalism. According to Peter Berger:

> The term globalization has come to be emotionally charged in public discourse. For some it implies the promise of an international civil society, conducive to a new era of peace and democratization. For others, it implies the threat of an American economic and political hegemony, with its cultural consequences being a homogenized world resembling a sort of metastasized Disneyland.[3]

If you were on the right side—namely, the American (Western) side—it was assumed that, forever, you would be on the winning side of a world that speaks your language and produces commodities that serve the American way of life. Consequently, most objections to the process of globalization centered on the victimization of developing countries. There was some truth to these descriptions (and there is still much to be said about the abuse of workers and national resources in developing economies); yet, critics failed to see that at the same time, in many parts of the developing world globalization created incentives not only to consume and supply cheap labor but also to create local industrial infrastructure and to cultivate human capital. East Asian states infused efforts in planning and funding national education systems that boost human skills. The results of such investments are reflected in the ranking offered by the international comparative tests. In the 2006 PISA (Programme for International Student Assessment) exam,[4] the top of the list was occupied by peripheral (except for Canada) Western states (Finland, Estonia, Australia) and signaled the emergence of new educational empires, all belonging to the Eastern Hemisphere: Japan, Singapore, Hong Kong, Taiwan, Korea, and China.

It suddenly became clear that the process of globalization was leading to unexpected consequences. It was no longer Western colonialism with an economic face—namely, a way to control and exploit markets and individuals unable to strike back. Rather, it created a global sphere where power traveled in different directions. Consequently, markets previously seen solely through the prism of economic opportunities began to be seen as a potential threat. The developed world discovered that it can be out-competed and that others can produce qualified, well-educated human capital that has an advantage not only over manual workers on the assembly lines or in call centers but also over doctors, engineers, and computer scientists. A new kind of competition evolved that touches the heart of the educated middle class.

A growing number of educated people in the East, equal in quality, much larger in quantity, and cheaper to employ, started undermining the competitive powers of the West. By the end of the twentieth century, it became clear that globalization embodies a threat to a wide range of social classes; from the poor, uneducated working class to middle-class college graduates, no one could be assured of remaining on the winning side of globalism.

The future of the developed world thus seemed far less glamorous. Members of the middle classes—who grow up believing that if they acquire a proper education they can expect to have a respectable job and be better off than their parents—now realize that despite their education, they too are exposed to the risks of the lower classes: unemployment, poverty, and homelessness. Even those who find a job are losing their ability to acquire the luxuries that during the last century had turned into necessities.

In the West, the new class of the educated poor keeps growing; even when employed, they hold part-time jobs or jobs that do not suit their qualifications. Not only do they earn less than they expected but less than what is necessary to maintain the kind of lifestyle they have experienced growing up.[5] In the last half century, processes of automation and computerization replaced, among others, receptionists, computer analysts, and doctors. The value of jobs demanding academic qualifications diminished, working conditions deteriorated, and the class of the educated poor expanded. In short, the global tsunami has reached the shores of the middle classes and swept them away.

The opposite process is taking place in Asian countries, where the middle classes are growing at a quicker pace than ever. The economy has moved from relying on unskilled cheap labor to focusing on highly skilled professional industries. Consequently, Asian economies offer an attractive combination of an unskilled, semiskilled, and a skilled workforce that attracts global investors. They are expanding their education in general and higher education in particular and establishing world-class research institutions that are out-competing their Western equivalents. It has been predicted that by the year 2050 the top Asian universities will be among the best in the world. The free world met the planned world and found out that it is losing its grip on excellence.[6]

The growing awareness that globalism is giving rise to more complex forms of competition and exploitation, creating a multitude of power centers whose members are qualified to play different roles—investors and inventors, business people, professionals and manual workers alike—transforms the picture of the future for those who used to consider their social position protected. A rift is being created between a thin elite secured in its privileged position and the middle classes for whom poverty is no longer a remote fear. It is this loss of personal security that motivates people to adopt a more national pattern of thinking: realizing they may not be able to do it on their own, they hope "we can do it together."

Their frustration is not the result of a manic state of mind or a misunderstanding of their interests; on the contrary, it is supported by hard evidence. The "Elephant Chart," based on data accumulated by the economist Branko Milanović, shows the distribution of global income growth between 1988 and 2008, a period that overlaps with the spread of Globalization 2.0 and 3.0. During this period the situation of the poor in developing countries improved, while the situation of the middle classes in developed countries deteriorated. Their future opportunities, and especially the opportunities of their children, are diminishing, becoming much less attractive. Without reading the recent McKinsey report, members of the middle classes already know that their children will be poorer than their parents.[7]

For some (a very small group of citizens of the developing countries) this is the best of times; for others it is the worst of times (at least in comparison to their experience and expectations in the previous thirty years). The most fortunate and the most vulnerable are citizens of the same countries. No wonder they have grown apart, with each class now holding its own map of future risks and opportunities that leads to a different reading

Global income growth, 1988-2008

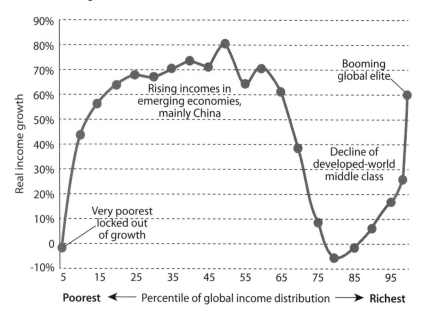

FIGURE 4. Global income growth. The *American Prospect* using data provided by Branko Milanović. Miles Corak, "The Winners and Losers of Globalization: Branko Milanović's New Book on Inequality Answers Two Important Questions," *American Prospect*, May 18, 2016.

of the future. The assumption that "we are in it together," which keeps social frameworks intact, is no longer credible. This is a global phenomenon. An international survey showed that

> between 65 and 70 percent of households in 25 advanced economies, the equivalent of 540 to 580 million people, were in segments of the income distribution whose real market income—their wages and income from capital—were flat or had fallen in 2014 in comparison with 2005. This compared with less than 2 percent, or fewer than 10 million people, who experienced this phenomenon between 1993 and 2005.[8]

When the elites are alienated from the needs and interests of the masses and, particularly, when they are endorsing self-serving policies, presenting them as a morally superior point of view, the claim—often described as reactionary or populist—that the elites do not represent the real interests of real people seems far truer and less demagogic than some would like us to believe.

Growing social gaps lead to the formation of separate, hostile identities; on the one side are those who experience a slowdown of social mobility, feeling locked within their socioeconomic positions, left out of the competitive game; on the other are those who have a secure place at the top. When the contours of success are shaped in ways that are open mostly to members of the elite, the formation of a real meritocracy is prevented, trust is eroded, and anger surfaces.

The fact that elites devote "considerable effort to cultivating their offspring's stock of academic currencies to ensure succession along kinship lines"[9] discloses the attempt to replace natural talent with breeding or, to use William Deresiewicz's term, with a "hereditary meritocracy."[10] Affluent parents, he argues, raise children who are "resume jockeys," prepared from early childhood to be admitted to the best schools and universities that will secure them prestigious jobs and high-level incomes. The elites welcome the exceptional few but block the way of perfectly able individuals whose parents lack the time and resources to breed them for acceptance. Those who make it to the top are taken to be proof that success is within reach. But it isn't. As social inequalities deepen, social mobility declines:

> One striking feature is the decline in upward mobility among middle-class workers, even those with college degree. Across the distribution of educational attainment, the likelihood of moving to the top deciles of the earnings distribution for workers who start

their career in the middle of the earning distribution has declined by approximately 20% since the early 1980s.[11]

Social immobility is enhanced by geographic separation, which, in turn, deepens feelings of estrangement and alienation. The life experiences of the different social groups vary, and there is very little social exchange across communities. Social differences are highlighted and used to raise social fences and make the price of crossing them higher. In another context I have called such moves "gap preserving policies," and though no one commends them publicly they are the motivating force behind many private and public policies. No wonder that social and economic gaps are growing faster than ever.[12]

From the perspective of the have-nots, the highly refined behavior of the upper classes and those who manage to join them is a form of dominance and supremacy. It is rejected not because it is deemed wrong, but because it is, for most, outside their reach. In his book *Hillbilly Elegy*, James David Vance argues that the hillbillies' resentment of Obama was an expression of such feelings. Obama was resented, he argues, because he was too perfect, too aloof, too unreachable, less of a role model and more of a source of irritation.

> The president feels like an alien to many Middletonians for reasons that have nothing to do with skin color. Recall that not a single one of my high school classmates attended an Ivy League school. Barack Obama attended two of them and excelled in both. He is brilliant, wealthy, and speaks like a constitutional law professor—which, of course, he is. Nothing about him bears any resemblance to the people I admired growing up: his accent—clear, perfect, neutral—is foreign: his credentials are so impressive that they're frightening... he conducts himself with a confidence that comes from knowing that the modern America meritocracy was built for him. . . .

President Obama came on the scene right as many people in my community began to believe that the modern American meritocracy was not built for them.

Barack Obama strikes at the heart of our deepest insecurities. He is a good father while many of us aren't. He wears suits to his job while we wear overalls, if we're lucky enough to have a job at all. His wife tells us that we shouldn't be feeding our children certain foods, and we hate her for it—not because we think she is wrong, but because we know she is right.[13]

This text captures the way social alienation turns into anger, resentment, and animosity. Contrary to the expectations of many, crossing the class line does not make one a local hero or a role model but "the other."[14]

The high correlation between socioeconomic background and educational achievements (at all levels of education) makes success class-based. Consequently, for some, poverty is a family heritage, while for others it is inherent wealth. When a class system turns into a caste system, it is not surprising that those left outside adopt a policy of "if you cannot join them beat them." The social protests now erupting around the world are less about gaining power and more about taking power away from those who seem to have betrayed their duty.

Living in different territories, cultivating different traditions, attending different educational institutions, confronting different dangers, inculcating different expectations, eating different kinds of foods, and facing different health problems and patterns of longevity, the different social classes develop separate identities and sets of values. The less well-off value tradition, place honor and duty high on their list of desirable virtues, and express a clearer national identity than members of the more affluent classes. Those who make it place freedom at the top of their list of priorities and articulate a greater attraction to the globalist vision.

Organized denial and ideological blindness leads the ruling elites to underestimate the importance of these divisive processes. They keep convincing themselves that ours is the best of times, an age of freedom and progress. A public speech delivered by Barack Obama in April 2016 captured the shortsightedness of the elites.

> We are fortunate to be living in the most peaceful, most prosperous, and most progressive era in human history. . . . It's been decades since the last war between major powers. More people live in democracies. We are wealthier and better educated, with a global economy that has lifted up more than a billion people from extreme poverty. . . . If you had to choose the moment in time to be born, any time in human history, and you didn't know ahead of time what nationality you were, or what gender or what your economic status might be, you'd choose today.[15]

This is the great speech of a global leader carrying the beacon of global prosperity and freedom. It is a less convincing message for many citizens who are experiencing the present as the worst of times, a time of personal and communal destitution. The speech highlights what I have been arguing thus far: the elites took a global leap forward and forgot to look at their political surroundings. Hence, they have broken the very first rule of social solidarity that lies at the heart of national and democratic beliefs: members must come first, not because they are in some inherent way better, but because we distribute what we have created together, and the way we distribute it reflects our collective will. This is the essence of the national-democratic contract. Taking care of each other is the norm—taking care of others is the exception.

16

The Birth of a Nationalist

In an article published following Brexit, Tony Blair, former British prime minister, divided the world into closed-minded and open-minded individuals: "the open-minded see globalization as an opportunity, with challenges that should be mitigated; the closed-minded see the outside world as a threat."[1] Blair is wrong to claim that the differences between nationalists and globalists reflect a difference in levels of moral development or state of mind. Being a nationalist or a globalist is not a constitutive state of mind; on the contrary, in light of changing circumstances, individuals locate themselves at different points along the global-national (G-N) continuum.

A 2016 global survey sheds new light on the correlation among education, rationality, and the way individuals position themselves on the G-N continuum.[2] The pollsters at GlobeScan questioned more than twenty thousand people in eighteen countries about their position. More than half of those living in emerging economies (such as Nigeria, China, Peru, and India) saw themselves as global rather than national citizens. The trend in the developed, industrialized, richer, and better educated nations seems to be heading in the opposite direction, with the concept of global citizenship appearing to have taken a serious hit after the financial crash of 2008. In Germany, for example, only 30 percent of respondents saw themselves as global citizens, the lowest percentage in fifteen years.

Are you a global citizen?

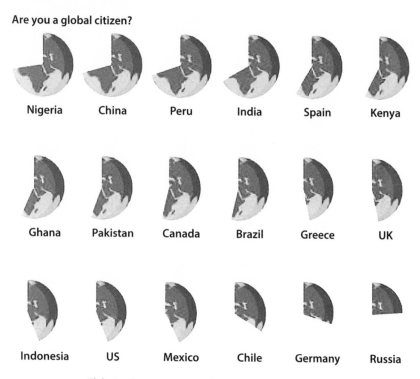

FIGURE 5. GlobeScan's 2016 survey on global citizenship. Source: GlobeScan poll for the BBC.

According to the survey, Nigerians are far more globally minded than Germans. The reason is not, however, that Nigerians are more rational, open-minded, or better educated than Germans, but rather that most of them see no future in their homeland and would like to be able to build their lives in a more prosperous society. The global perspective makes it clear that one's position on the G-N continuum reflects his/her evaluation of his/her individual and collective life chances. Rational calculations influence the tendency of the more educated and economically established to place themselves closer to the G pole and of the less educated and more economically vulnerable to position themselves at the opposite pole.

Globalists wish to convince individuals that national affiliations have a diminishing influence on their risks and opportunities, hence they would like individuals to be looking beyond the nation-state into a global world where nothing counts but talent and will. This is a naive and misleading point of view. Considering that less than 4 percent of the world's population are immigrants (living in a country they were not born in), the assumption that one's life chances are independent of one's country of origin is deceptive. Most people's lives are state-centered, so investing in the well-being of our nation-state is not a sign of sentimental unreasonableness but of a rational evaluation of the best means of promoting our goals. In fact, most of us have as good a reason to invest in improving our collective well-being as in bettering our own personal welfare. The national way of thinking reflects this reality. Is it any wonder that so many people are drawn to it?

The bottom line is clear: Individuals are better off if they structure their preferences in light of actual risks and opportunities. Wartime is a good example; being exposed to common existential risks diminishes the importance of personal difference; hence, individuals tend to lean toward the national pole. In times of peace and prosperity, social cohesion is eroded and individuals are inclined to endorse a more global and universal point of view. The answer to the often-raised question, why cannot we stick together in good times as much as in bad ones, is simple: because it is against our best interests.

Obviously, social and economic circumstances aren't the only factors that affect a person's scheme of risks and opportunities. When membership in a racial, ethnic, gender, or religious group determines one's fate, the importance of other kinds of social differences is being marginalized. The case of German Jews living under the Nazi regime is a clear example of the way extreme circumstances erased in-group differences and clustered all members into one consolidated "risk group." Before the Nazi era, German Jews were not at all united. Many were in the midst of assimilating; in fact, quite a number believed they had already assimilated. They also differed in their human capital, financial wealth, and social position as well as in their religious and national preferences: some held cosmopolitan views and some were German patriots, while others had turned to Zionism. The Nazi regime erased their individual capital and made their risks and opportunities dependent solely on their national-religious identity. At that particular point in history, being Jewish was all that mattered. A miscalculation of one's risks and opportunities or an evaluation that relied on assumptions that were no longer relevant had fatal implications; many of those who assumed that their wealth or skills would save them ended up in the gas chambers.

One may never be in a situation where it is advisable to choose the N pole or the G pole; this is not a reflection of one's moral qualities but of the life experiences imposed on the person despite his/her will. This claim raises questions concerning moral luck. The moral tests we face are often determined by factors that are beyond our control:

> It may be true of someone that in a dangerous situation he would behave in a cowardly or heroic fashion, but if the situation never arises, he will never have the chance to distinguish or disgrace himself in this way, and his moral record will be different.[3]

We tend to ignore external circumstances and judge people "for what they actually do or fail to do, not just for what they would have done if circumstances had been different."[4] This biases our judgment against individuals forced to cope with more demanding external conditions.

A discussion of moral luck may seem to bear the mark of social determinism. This is not necessarily true; it is reasonable to assume that people are free to choose how to act in any given circumstance, yet it is only natural that their decisions would reflect their self-interest. Attitudes toward immigration or affirmative action may highlight the case in question. Many of those who support progressive immigration policies will encounter immigrants only as cheap service providers or laborers, while many of those who wish to restrict immigration will compete with immigrants for a part-time job, or see the value of their property decline as immigrants move into their neighborhood. Apparently, those who support progressive immigration policies have less of a reason to be concerned with the impact of immigration on their daily life than those who wish to restrict immigration. Are those who are "pro-immigration" better people than those who wish to restrict immigration? I doubt it.

Good luck does not reflect good character; think of wealthy people celebrated for their generous donations (often regardless of the way they have earned their fortune); are they better people than a poor person who shares a meal with someone in need? Probably not, yet the poor person will rarely be noticed. The fact that we are products not only of our own free will but also of our external circumstances points to the importance of the combination of freedom and fate that structures our private and communal lives.

It is evident that the general economic and political state of affairs influences the way people evaluate their risks and opportunities. In times of prosperity, when growth is assumed to produce more for everyone, people are more generous and open-minded; in times of austerity, when the economy slows down, people assume that things will get worse, that their risks will mount and their opportunities will shrink; they are therefore more protective of their interests and less inclined to support policies that would intensify competition.

When economic optimism reigns and progress seems inevitable, it is reasonable to follow the "Lockean proviso," according to which individuals have the right to acquire as much private property as they can (mostly land in Locke's days), as long as what they leave behind for others is enough and "as good."[5] The moral assumption is simple (maybe simplistic): cultivating one's talents will create more goods to be enjoyed by all; leaving enough for others ensures that they too can carve a qualitative piece out of these goods. Provided everybody has enough, it will be fair if the diligent and creative have more.

The impact of the Lockean proviso on modern thinking cannot be overestimated. Even though Lockean conditions of abundance no longer exist, the idea that having more as a result of hard work is not unfair, and that envy, in and of itself, is unjustified has deeply influenced modern conceptions of justice. But what happens if there simply isn't enough for everyone? Locke's assumptions are reversed in times of austerity. Expecting there will be less to share, we must be much more careful with the way goods are distributed, making sure that what is left for others is indeed qualitative and good enough. Caring about others' wealth thus turns from a matter of pure envy into a way of securing future needs. No wonder that the haves are eager to convince the public that growth and progress are endless while the have-nots warn against the dangers embedded in austerity. If the former are right, then we should all be envy-free; if the latter describe social reality in more adequate terms, then each and every one of us must fight to secure her/his need.

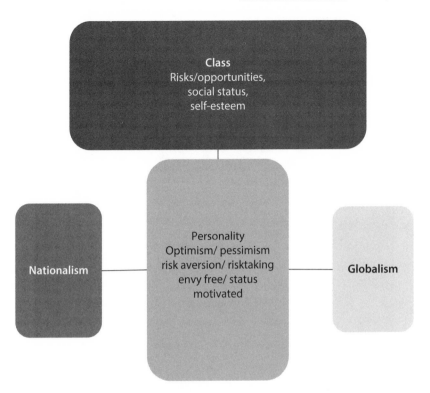

FIGURE 6. Proposed model of the G-N continuum.

The claim that one's stand in the G-N debate correlates with one's circumstances may irritate nationalists and globalists alike; both would prefer to present their position as normative rather than instrumental. If the difference between the two points of view has little to do with holding the right set of moral values, then neither can claim moral superiority or aspire to convince others to join its camp, as such a move will demand not merely a change of heart but also of one's life chances.[6]

Figure 6 summarizes the argument, showing that individuals move along the G-N continuum, positioning themselves at different spots due to a complex calculation of their risks and opportunities (also mediated by their personality).

My argument thus suggests that changing social and economic circumstances causes individuals around the world to reevaluate their risks and opportunities, leading many to assume that putting their nation first will best serve their interests. The time is therefore ripe for the emergence of a new kind of nationalism that is rational and well calculated.

17

The Nationalism of the Vulnerable

We already have some explanations for the question, why would the vulnerable adopt nationalism as their preferred strategy? The answer marries the economic crisis with a crisis of identity. The roots of this state of affairs are to be found somewhere at the very end of the last century—a growing sense of self-satisfaction led liberal democratic nation-states to passivity. With no ideological enemies to fight they allowed themselves to let go of some of the most valuable tools of nation building.

To members of the majority, nationalism became transparent. The national assets became so invisible that many believed liberal democratic states were morally and culturally neutral. At first liberals were surprised when minorities complained that the particular culture, tradition, or religion characteristic of the public sphere alienates them and discriminates against them. Yet twenty years of identity conflicts ended in victory—the rebellion of the minorities added to the public discourse terms such as *cultural domination* and *cultural exploitation*. Nonrecognition was acknowledged as a form of oppression and disrespect. Cultural recognition turned into a human right.[1]

Looking at the world from their secure position, liberals felt safe in allowing newcomers and those previously excluded to partake in structuring a far more diverse and open public sphere. Aware of the oppressive nature of the power of majorities, walking a thin line between toleration and domination, they agreed to share their public assets. Diversity flourished. In America, Mark Lilla argues, this process of abdication started when liberals "threw themselves into the movement politics of identity, losing a sense of what we share as citizens and what binds us as a nation. An image for Roosevelt liberalism and the unions that supported it was that of two hands shaking. A recurring image of identity liberalism is that of a prism refracting a single beam of light into its constituent colors, producing a rainbow. This says it all."[2]

The most significant change happened in schools and academic institutions that were no longer called on to make and remake the national narrative but rather to be critical, open-minded, and pluralistic. The same academic fields that fostered the national narrative were now happy to highlight its fictitious roots and exclusionary nature.[3] The consensual narrative started to be questioned, and each minority culture, ethnicity, race, color, or gender was encouraged to voice its own version of history, culture, traditions, and norms. National unity was eroded and pluralism replaced the "melting pot" policy. This was a liberating moment, but a price tag was attached to it. The newly emerging rainbow coalition was colorful and attractive; it stressed internal differences, yet it made the notion of a national collective very ambiguous. Ambiguity calls for a struggle, and each and every group felt this was the moment to try and imprint the public sphere with its particular qualities. In order to do so, minority groups attempted to crystallize their identity, making it richer and more distinct than all others.

As long as the theme was remembered, social, political, and economic variety made life richer, more interesting. Yet, in time, the different narratives started competing for primacy, and the newly established harmony turned into cacophony. While it would have been natural for the majority to fight back in order to restore balance, members of the elite were more interested in securing their place in the global world than in remaking the nation. The mobile members of the majority thus lost (some would say surrendered) their position of leadership. While minorities were consolidating their identity, the defining features of the majority started to fade; soon they become known as those who do not carry any specific identity. In Canada, for example, they are defined as "the rest of Canada" (as opposed to those in Quebec with its clear cultural and linguistic identity); in Spain they are the rest of Spain (as opposed to those in Catalonia and the Basque country). In other places the majorities adopted the identity of the megacities they inhabited, being Tel-Avivians, New Yorkers, Londoners, or Berliners, rather than Israeli, American, English, or German.

Weak members of the majority were left behind; they inhabited the mainland and the rural areas; the megacities and coastal areas were foreign to them. In this new world, being what they are—white, male, members of a majority—was to be apologizing for the privileges you do not have, to be forced to give way to others, be pushed back by those defended by affirmative action. To be situated in a defensive position while your social networks are falling apart, your income has stagnated (if not decreased), your children are worse off, and your life expectancy drops is a reasonable source of anger.

Feeling excluded and deprived, those left behind wish to revive the traditional social and national contours that provided them with a well-defined and privileged identity. In the heydays of the nation-state they could have recruited the elites for this purpose, but nowadays the elites are less keen to define themselves in national terms and have left national terminology and symbols for the vulnerable to adopt. Can it be any surprise that the vulnerable claim to be the true representatives of the nation?

The vulnerable are not territorially concentrated and they do not share a distinct language, culture, or history, so they tend to define themselves in sentimental terms. They cling to a nostalgic memory of "the good old days" when their nation gave them a sense of dignity. Being unable to be proud of themselves, they emphasize the shortcomings of others that disrupted the traditional way of life that afforded them a comfortable social place. Consequently, their self-definition is grounded in exclusionary ideas, often sliding into xenophobia, racism, and misogyny, negative perspectives that help them cope with their hardships. While their aspiration to secure for themselves the privileges they had is unjustified, their demand to be equally treated, not to be ignored and left behind, deserves careful attention.

The disintegration of the majority, the fact that it is divided into separate socioeconomic groups who share no common fate or culture, erodes feelings of belonging and isolates members from their reference group. The less successful parts of the faceless majority seek support by recruiting two players, a team that played well in the past and won many victories: God and the nation. Recounting the mood among hillbillies, Vance describes his grandmother's set of beliefs. She "always had two Gods: Jesus Christ and the United States of America, I was no different, and neither was anyone else I know."[4] No wonder religious fundamentalism and extreme right-wing nationalism simultaneously reappear. History teaches us that there is no social, cultural, and political vacuum. When the elites lose their desire to nurture the nation, when liberal democrats surrender their educative mission, others fill their place.

Having lost their protected social status, the vulnerable find themselves at the bottom of the social heap. Worse still, their plight attracts ridicule rather than empathy. Rejected and locked into their social position, they feel hurt and angry. In *Strangers in Their Own Land: Anger and Mourning on the American Right*, Arlie Hochschild travels deep into what is known as "Trump Land," meeting good people swamped by anger, despair, and deep pessimism. They regard the liberal talk on progress and diversity as deceptive "mumbo jumbo" and distrust the elites and the federal government.[5]

They are sad and pessimistic. A Pew Economic Mobility Project studying how Americans evaluate their economic risks and opportunities shows that "there is no group of Americans more pessimistic than working class whites."[6] While the majority of blacks, Latinos, and college-educated whites expect their children to do better than they did, "among working class whites, only 44% share that expectation . . . and 42% of working class whites report that their lives are less economically successful than those of their parents."[7]

Being pushed out of the social reselling ring is bad enough; being blamed for your failure makes things even worse. Being members of the majority, the vulnerable are expected to take responsibility for their lives. A failure to do so is taken to be a result of one's own doing. In *The Working Poor: Invisible in America*, David K. Shipler contends that the "American Myth" (replicated in most Christian countries) provides a justification for laying the blame for poverty on the poor.

> In the Puritan legacy, hard work is not merely practical but also moral; its absence suggests an ethical lapse. A harsh logic dictates a hard judgment: if a person's diligent work leads to prosperity, if work is a moral virtue, and if anyone in the society can attain

prosperity through work, then the failure to do so is a fall from righteousness. In the American atmosphere, poverty has always carried a whiff of sinfulness.[8]

True to the naive and self-serving belief that those who work hard are rewarded for their efforts, poverty, especially white poverty, is taken to be a sign of personal misdemeanor. The poor, it is argued, own their poverty just as much as the rich own their property.

This is not just an American point of view; all over the world the poor are stereotyped in similar ways. A Save the Children Fund study conducted in Britain shows that the poor are seen as irresponsible, having too many children, lazy, reluctant to work, disposed to cheat the system in order to get undeserved benefits, unmotivated, politically illiterate, or simply dumb.[9] Media reports of poverty often include references to antisocial behavior, which add to the feeling that the principle of deservingness is particularly conspicuous.

Poor whites thus remain the one group it is still legitimate to label. A philosopher friend shared the following telling anecdote: Editors of a prestigious academic journal accepted a paper on humor and stereotyping for publication. The paper opened with the following joke: "Why can't Stevie Wonder read? Because he is black." They rejected it, feeling the joke painted the journal in a racist light, and decided to exchange it with the following joke:

> A brain transplant patient is offered a choice between two types of brains. The doctor tells him, "We have a normal brain for $5,000 and a Redneck brain for $10,000." "Why are Redneck brains twice as expensive as normal brains?" he asks in amazement. The doctor replies, "Well, they are brand new—they have never been used."[10]

This is a superb example of the way the liberal bias in favor of diversity and against poor whites plays itself out. It is particularly poignant, because the editors of the journal see themselves as progressives who despise racism and chauvinism. While they find jokes about blacks disturbing they are less concerned about rednecks. As Vance painfully concluded:

> White trash is the one ethnic group it is still OK to make fun of. . . . And if you're an elite white professional, working-class, whites are an easy target: You don't have to feel guilty for being a racist or a xenophobe. By looking down on the Hillbilly, you can get that high of self-righteousness and superiority without violating any of the moral norms of your own tribe.[11]

Social dismissal causes pain and anger; the people Hochschild interviewed are well aware of the fact that "liberals think that Bible-believing Southerners are ignorant, backward, Rednecks, losers. They think we are racist, sexist, homophobic and maybe fat." "I am not sure they are wrong," one of her interviewees says, "but even if they are, the feeling of being looked down on is a devastating one."[12] As social and economic alienation takes root, contempt between members of the majority surges; progressives take hillbillies to be worthy of disdain, while hillbillies see the metropolitan liberals as an untrustworthy, self-interested, selfish lot who raped the country (and them) of its riches.

The vulnerable are offended that members of the elite do not try to understand their pain. Being so lightly dismissed they assume they have nothing to offer but their misery. There is no glory in poverty, and no one really wants to be identified with it or befriend it. In the preamble of his book, Vance explains that he writes in order to give "his people" a voice:

> I want people to understand what happens in the life of the poor and the psychological impact that spiritual and material poverty has on their children. . . . I may be white, but I do not identify with the

WASPs of the Northeast. Instead, I identify with the millions of working class white Americans of Scots-Irish descent who have no college degree. To these folks poverty is a family tradition. Americans call them Hillbillies, Rednecks, or White Trash. I call them neighbors, friends and family.[13]

The move from being working class to being poor is devastating. It is well reflected in the discomfort Vance felt at Yale (his alma mater) in comparison to the way the British writer Margaret Foster felt at Oxford in the 1960s. To her surprise, she discovered that "being working class . . . was the thing . . . instead of being embarrassed by our class, or concealing it, we flaunted it, to great effect, realizing how special it made us . . . working class became fashionable."[14] Almost half a century and an ocean apart, Foster's experience fundamentally differs from that of Vance. As Foster recalls, some grandeur was associated with the notion of the "working classes," while none is associated with being poor. Working-class people are perceived as diligent, self-supporting, dignified, unspoiled by wealth and uncorrupted by the pursuit of pleasure; the poor are seen as lazy, loud, vulgar, and often repellent. The poor would have liked to emphasize other qualities like honor, courage, or family, local and national loyalties, but adhering to such national traits makes them seem anachronistic if not reactionary. They are therefore on the lookout for a more satisfying self-definition.

Class has its heroes, its representatives, its demands, and most of all the ability to organize. The poor are unorganized, underrepresented, and often ashamed of their social standing. Surrendering the energizing and motivating "class talk" thus leaves the poor neglected, ignored, disregarded, with nothing to rely on. The poor are stripped of role models; they do not have a Martin Luther King, Cornel West, or Barack Obama to represent their cause, neither do they have literary figures such as Virginia Woolf and Sylvia Plath or inspirational theorists such as Iris Young, Carol Gilligan, or Martha Nussbaum to organize their resistance. "We never looked at our parents as role models and actually I don't think they wanted us to, I think they wanted us to go on, do something different," says one of the interviewees in Selina Todd's *The People: The Rise and Fall of the Working Class*.[15] Those who make it move on; those left behind are deprived of the chance of being valued for who they are.

The individualization of poverty sets our way of thinking about the present social challenges as well as of the range of desirable solutions. It is particularly poisonous in the age of identity politics. As the burdens involved in being a minority were recognized, social and political moves were taken to alleviate it. Women, people of color, immigrants, alongside members of other minority groups, could thus refer to their identity in order to vindicate their social position, but male members of the majority were held accountable—not to say culpable—for their misfortune. The less well-off members of the majority saw "others" being helped while they were criticized and scorned for their misery.

The crystallization of the vulnerable into an identity group went unnoticed until the liberal progressive camp started losing one election campaign after the other. This wasn't, as many assumed, a moment of democratic crisis but of democratic victory, not because the people elected were democratic champions but because certain social trends that had previously been silenced suddenly got a voice. Democracy was now fulfilling its assigned role, highlighting the importance of unattended social and political issues.

The elites were shaken and traumatized because they did not see it coming; they failed to see how a growing segment of their fellow nationals were losing control over their lives. They convinced themselves that while social inequality is a major feature of contemporary Western societies, class struggles have been eradicated. The British example is the most poignant one. In the 1950s and 1960s class occupied a major role in British political discourse; this prominence faded away in the 1980s. By the end of the 1990s an unusual consensus evolved between John Major (the Conservative prime minister) and Tony Blair (the subsequent Labor prime minister): Britain had become a classless society. During this period class consciousness was eroded, and the British working class was individualized and de-organized, losing its pride, its glory, and its trade unions. Yet social stratification intensified, and those at the bottom had no illusion that a new definition would improve their life chances.

The elimination of class from the social and the political discourse freed the elites from offering ways of closing income gaps, allowing neoliberalism to be solidified, convincing the public (and themselves) that the liberal economic model, including the extreme accumulation of wealth in the hands of the few, is socially beneficial for all. At the end of the day, it was assumed, wealth will trickle down and help move the economy forward, thus improving the quality of life for all members, including the worse off.

According to Joseph Stiglitz, who is no stranger to the role of the elites in shaping the economic debate of the last decades, "the powerful manipulate public perception by appeals to fairness and efficiency while the real outcomes benefit only them."[16] Warren Buffett is blunter: "There's been class warfare going on for the last 20 years and my class has won."[17] The victory of the elites over the working classes was framed as a celebration of progress, pluralism, and diversity; the losers were supposed to rejoice too.

The move to multiculturalism was a convenient distraction, drawing attention toward cultural differences and away from class-based conflicts. The more diversity blind a society became the less able it was able to capture the discriminating power of class. The whole idea of grouping people along the lines of gender, race, ethnicity, or sexual preferences was that these identities transcend class differences. What was taken to be true of minorities was assumed to be true also of the majority. This lessened awareness of poignant dilemmas such as who should get more social support and protection, poor whites or middle-class minority members.[18]

The move to identity politics allowed the elites to pick and choose those who joined their ranks: Women were the first to make good use of equal opportunities. When official barriers were removed, enough middle-class women who had been well cultivated, sharing the elite culture and set of values, were ready to join the race. Members of other groups adopted the same path of integration. Those who wanted to fit in had to change, adopting habits, norms, tastes, culinary preferences, and the political lingo of the ruling classes with a feminist, black, or gay twist.

The elites rightly assumed that adopting diversity or multiculturalism was far less costly than advancing a class-based social change. Admitting skillful members of minority groups and letting them prosper within existing frameworks was a less demanding social move than sharing resources with the have-nots. Consequently, the last half of the twentieth century opened up new opportunities to some very able women and the most talented members of minority groups. Exceptional individuals made it all the way to the White House, but racial gaps remained a sore issue; outstanding women were elected to run the world's banking system and head governments and international corporations, yet women remain among the poorest members of every society.

These processes turned the talent pyramid upside down: the gaps between the opportunities of exceptionally talented members of previously excluded groups and mediocre members of the elite were closing down. This doomed mediocre members of both minority groups and lower social economic strata to failure. A lot of talent was lost. Under the banner of meritocracy, "social and economic inequalities deepen and the idea of equal opportunities is ridiculed.[19] The poor met the "class ceiling." Even though levels of education (measured by years of schooling, rate of graduation, and enrollment in higher-education institutions) reached unprecedented heights, social mobility slowed down. It has become clear that education can no longer be the magic panacea, as it fails to reduce social and economic inequalities; in fact, it often reproduces and intensifies them. The haves are opting out of the national education system and into private ones, structuring a distinct social and cultural experience for their children; the rest are left with a dilapidated public education system that cannot serve their needs.[20]

In America a sense of helplessness, associated with a sense of social loneliness and a lack of cross-class solidarity, allowed for the emergence of two unusual candidates, Bernie Sanders and Donald Trump, both willing to challenge the ruling social norms and place the socially displaced at the center of his campaign. While Sanders invoked class issues, Trump played the national card, and both pierced the thin crust covering liberal hypocrisy toward globalism, an ideology justified by universal values that benefited a few at the expense of many. Social frustration released a repressed nationalist voice. To the great disappointment of those who believed that the class war was over; it is now reappearing, wearing a national gown.

The strong affinity between class and national choices is a worldwide phenomenon. Brexit made it clear that class differences play a prominent role in determining peoples' minds, social and economic status highly correlated with voters' positions on the Remain-Leave continuum (which parallels the Globalism-Nationalism continuum previously discussed).[21] The morning after Brexit, Fiona Trott from Hartlepool in northeast England was neither surprised nor disappointed. Although the town had benefited from international investments, seven out of ten residents backed Brexit. She explained it as "a vote against the establishment. Unemployment is 9.4%. People feel hard done by. When you stop and talk to voters in the street, they tell you things couldn't get any worse, so why not vote for change?" In Dudley, a town near Birmingham, some of the poorest areas voted by the largest margin (68 percent) to leave, and working-class Labor voters in Wales voted "Leave" against their party line.[22] The very same morning, at Oxford University, people were shocked to find out that they had lost the vote. Not surprisingly, the farther away you were from the university, the more likely it was that you voted Leave. For many Remain supporters, the day after Brexit felt like waking up in a foreign land. The "other country" was a few blocks away; "town and gown" were more divided than ever.

Why did social frustration translate into conservative anti-European or a nationalist sentiment rather than support for the Labor party and the welfare state? The answer reflects the fact that the leadership of the British Labor party, like many other progressive leaders around the world, was closer to the elites than to the people. For many liberal, progressive leaders even a small dose of patriotism was too much, not because they were indifferent to the well-being of their fellow nationals but because they feared the slippery slope of racism, xenophobia, Islamophobia, anti-immigration policies, and the like. Yet the slope is slippery on both sides; the other side leads to neoliberalism, globalism, and ultimately social alienation and the collapse of social solidarity. There is a clear need to restore the balance.

In its prime, nationalism was "the great equalizer"; it turned subjects into citizens, motivated the construction of an inclusive public sphere, and inspired the creation of a comprehensive education system and a shared language that promoted a fusion of high and low cultures into one national culture to be enjoyed by all members. Above all, it gave individuals a place in the world they could call their own.

In our global world it is often assumed that it is better to be free than equal, to cross national boundaries than feel at home; hence the social, political, and economic goods nationalism offered seem outdated. But they are not; those feeling exposed, unable to secure a decent life for themselves and their children, would like to revive them. They have secured a significant victory with political attention having been given to their claims. To the dismay of the elites, in the near future, we are therefore likely to hear more about the need to re-create a new national cross-class coalition and about the benefits of nationalism.

Those adopting the global point of view claim that "Putting America First" is a fascist slogan, identical to "Germany Above All Else"; they are mistaken. Rather than expressing a sense of supremacy, this slogan articulates a desire to regenerate a sense of commitment among fellow nationals. And there are many ways of putting one's nation first: Bernie Sanders's call to America's billionaire class—"you cannot continue to take advantage of all the benefits of America, if you refuse to accept your responsibilities"—is one option; John F. Kennedy's famous summons: "Ask not what your country can do for you, ask what you can do for your country" is another. Theresa May's statement that "citizens of the world are citizens of nowhere," and Macron's description of his debate with Marine Le Pen as a debate between "patriotism and nationalism" all testify that a new wave of nationalism is here.

A paradigm shift has occurred; it is now clear that elites have been using a social and economic prism that distorted their view, preventing them from seeing what they should have seen, leading them to misinterpret reality. Going global over the head of their own fellow national was a moral and democratic mistake. No democracy can survive without the firm support of the elites and upper middle classes. We must then shed new light on national sentiments; rather than seeing nationalism as the last refuge of the scoundrel we should start thinking of nationalism as the last hope of the needy.

Historically, nationalism filtered down from the elites to the people; now it has changed direction, representing grassroots feelings and demands. It will ally with those who give it a hand. If liberal forces want to re-recruit "the people" they should reconsider where they want to be placed on the N-G continuum. Their present interests pull in the global direction, but understanding the long-term consequences of neoliberal globalism may lure them to move back in the opposite direction.

Globalization complicated the choices of the elites. Dani Rodrik describes the political trilemma caused by hyperglobalization: hyperglobalization, he argues, is incompatible with democracy. We need then to decide. Rodrik's preference is clear: "democracy and national self-determination should trump hyper-globalization. Democracies have the right to protect their social arrangements, and when this clashes with the requirements of global economy, it is the latter that should give way.[23] It is not the first time democracy and nationalism are on the same side of the fence. Once this realization sinks in, our choices will be much simpler.

18

The Nationalism of the Affluent

The crumbling down of the modern nation-state succumbing to the pressures of globalism on the one hand and localism on the other is also the origin of the second kind of nationalism. When political power is eroded and the state faces a legitimization crisis, members of minority nations are lured to question the existing national/political status quo. Yet, unlike the nationalism of the vulnerable that seeks to strengthen the nation-state, separatist nationalism wishes to seize the moment and loosen existing political frameworks. In so doing it harks back to twentieth-century claims of national self-determination pointing to the historical injustice done to small nations who were never allowed to enjoy equal opportunities and were forced to merge into larger political frameworks that eradicated their unique identity.

Inhabiting a distinct territory and sharing a common history, culture, and language, members of small nations turn to their distinct identity to justify their demand for self-rule. As a standard type of nationalism, separatism aims to recruit the support of all fellow nationals, thus forming a cross-class coalition. In this sense it is an inclusive kind of nationalism that labors to make its reference group as large and prosperous as possible. Hence, for liberals, the political language separatists speak is much more palatable than that of the vulnerable—this, however, does not mean that separatist claims are more justified or applicable than other nationalist claims.

Presently, the most visible case of national separatism is that of Catalonia, but the Catalans are not alone. The creation of the European Union shifted power away from individual states to the European community; for members of small nations, being part of a particular nation-state thus became less of an asset (sometimes a burden). This inspired small nations to claim the independence they were refused. Consequently, separatist movements from the northern parts of Italy (Lombardy and Veneto) to Flanders, Scotland, the Faroe Islands, South Tirol, Corsica, and Kurdistan are gathering momentum, challenging the integrity of existing nation-states, demanding to carve for themselves an independent cultural and political sphere.

Their claims force us to reexamine the birth of many of the modern nation-states, understanding why in the age of national self-determination so few nations were able to realize this vision, why there was "only one effective nationalism for ten potential ones."[1] The answer teaches us an important lesson regarding the nature of nationalism and its interaction with other political theories.

The story of the small nations makes it clear that national arguments cannot survive on their own; their power comes from the ability to serve the needs of the emerging modern state. The nation had to help establish a state that could be, if not prosperous, then at least viable. The basic assumption was that for modern states to function well they must be able to form a sizeable economy, have defensible borders, and nurture a prosperous cultural life. Nations that were too small to supply these elementary goods could not pass the threshold of self-determination. The desire to overlap national aspirations with considerations of viability meant that small national groups were forced to join a large political framework. National movements gaining independence were therefore movements of national unification.

Germany, France, and Italy (to mention a few) grew out of a merger of different national groups: Bretons, Normands, and Corsicans became French; Bavarians, North Westphalians, and Brandenburgians became German; and Sicilians, Lombardians, and Emilia Romagnians turned Italian.[2] The result was that, like a Russian doll, each modern nation-state contained within itself a smaller nation(s). Which was the "real" nation? The definitional ambiguity of the term left the question open and the debate unresolved.

The "threshold of state viability" was defined by Friedrich List. For nations to be able to prosper, he claimed, they must have a large population and an extensive territory endowed with manifold national resources; these, he concluded, were the essential requirements of normal nationality.

> A nation restricted in the number of its population and in territory, especially if it has a separate language, can only possess a crippled literature and crippled institutions for promoting art and science. A small state can never bring to complete perfection within its territory the various branches of production.[3]

The assertion that nations that fall below a critical mass have no historical justification for self-determination shattered the political dreams of the small nations, condemning them to social, cultural, and political annihilation.[4] List acknowledged the fact that, "There were too many of them [nations],"[5] and some were condemned to oblivion. This was not taken to be a pressing moral or political difficulty or a violation of national or individual rights but a reflection of "moral luck," "the order of nature," "the survival of the fittest."

Taking for granted that a viable high culture sustaining a modern state and a modern economy "cannot fall below a certain minimal size, and that there is room for only a limited number of states on this earth," the merging of small nations into larger ones was portrayed as a necessity, a victory of utilitarianism over nationalism. This is well expressed in the work of the British philosopher John Stuart Mill. Despite his enthusiastic support for self-rule and national self-determination, Mill was convinced that the assimilation of smaller nations into bigger ones was no more than a blessing:

> Nobody can suppose that it is not more beneficial for a Breton or a Basque of French Navarre to be a member of the French nationality . . . than to sulk on his own rocks, the half-savage relic of past times, revolving in his own little mental orbit, without participation or interest in the general movement of the world. The same remark applies to the Welshman or the Scottish highlander as members of the British nation.[6]

Needless to say, neither the Basques, the Scots, nor members of any other small nation accepted this description, but they were on the wrong side of history.

Given the power of utilitarian arguments to determine the construction of future states, why didn't they replace nationalism as a ruling ideology? The answer sends us back to the opening chapters of this book: the maximization of utilitarian considerations—be they political, economic, or cultural— cannot serve as a good enough political justification for the establishment of independent political units. Modern states aspire to ground their existence in arguments that go beyond utility, or else their legitimacy will be questioned if and when their functionality is eroded.

Utilitarian arguments are never conclusive and cannot answer the most basic question of all: whose utility are we seeking to maximize? Obviously, different individuals, regions, and local units evaluate utility differently. Think, for example, of the

Northern League advocating the creation of a new state for Italy's wealthier regions, wishing to free itself from the burdens of the poorer south. Utility calculations of the north collide with those of other regions and of the Italian state as a whole. Who is to judge which one of the conflicting interests should take priority over the others? One could obviously try to develop tools of optimization, maximizing the utility of the greater number of individuals, but then why stop at the Italian border rather than looking across it?

The case of the Donetsk People's Republic, which, following a referendum, declared independence from the Ukraine, sharpens the dilemma of whose interests determine the future of a land: those inside the contested area, those nearby, or anyone else who has a vested interest. The more disputed an issue is, the less likely it is to find an adequate democratic or utilitarian answer.

Moreover, as utilitarian arguments are grounded in particular circumstances, when these change they produce new answers to old questions. Once again Europe is an excellent example: the emergence of the European Union changed the balance of utilitarian arguments, undermining the importance of the viability argument. Thus, contrary to the expectations of its founders, the European Union did not lead to postnationalism but to the reemergence of small nations' nationalism. Indeed, today's separatist nationalism is the nationalism of small affluent nations that were oppressed by the threshold principle and were excluded from the national discourse not because they lacked national spirit but because of utilitarian considerations. They are now setting out to gain self-determination, aspiring to free themselves of the nation-state they were forced to join and revive their historical national identity. Yet their states would not let them go.

Quite confusingly, in these separatist debates the term *nation* is used on both sides of the fence: the Spanish nation-state and the Catalan region, the Belgian state and Flanders, Italy and Lombardy—all claim the title of *nation*, thus revealing the multinational character of nation-states. Section II of the Spanish Constitution explicitly expresses this complexity, emphasizing the fact that the Spanish nation is "the common and indivisible homeland of all Spaniards." Yet it also "recognizes and guarantees the right to self-government of the nationalities and regions of which it is composed and the solidarity among them all."[7] Why must Spain be taken to be "indissoluble" and "indivisible"? Why cannot this unity be questioned? These questions are raised by the Catalans, the Basques, the Lombards, the Scots, leaving the old nation-states speechless as they witness their own national arguments being used against them.

What is there to be found at the end of a slippery slope that starts with challenging the unity of existing political units? Here is a somewhat comic but in another sense challenging answer: Those opposing the demands of Catalonia for independence have created Tabarnia, a fictitious region that wants independence from Catalonia. Initiated in the broad coastal strip that stretches from Tarragona to Barcelona, Tabarnia "is a good-humored backlash against what many see as the imposition of an independence agenda on a part of Catalonia that has never voted for secessionist candidates." Tabarnia went viral, gaining the support of tens of thousands of individuals who signed a petition in favor of its independence, using the same arguments and language as the Catalonians use against Spain. Their slogan—"Barcelona is not Catalonia"—echoes the secessionists' own "Catalonia is not Spain. "Tabarnia claims that the Barcelona area does not benefit from the wealth the city creates, much as Catalan separatists complain the region contributes more to the

Spanish state than it gets back."[8] And Tabarnia isn't the end of it; the Balkanization of states and regions could be endless, and none is protected from challenges to its unity.

As the threshold argument is no longer effective, the only other utilitarian argument that comes to the rescue of larger nation-states is *state integrity*. Being afraid of the process of Balkanization, the European Union now made it axiomatic; the EU is reluctant to recognize new states, even if, as in the case of Kosovo, NATO was involved in forcing Serbia to withdraw from its territories in order to allow it to gain independence. The European Commission adheres to the Prodi doctrine, arguing "that a breakaway state should have to leave the bloc and could then be let back only if it had gained independence in accordance with the constitutional law of the member state it left." Moreover, in order to join the union, any new state must win "the unanimous agreement of all others."[9] These declarations are meant to mellow separatist aspirations, warning small nations they would be left on their own, unable to enjoy the protective umbrella of the union.

And yet separatists still feel this is the right moment to tackle the weakening state. Motivated by their relative affluence, they fight to secure their members' prosperity and to be freed from their social and economic obligations to less affluent regions, keeping the fruits of social production within their territory. Once again it becomes obvious that one's place along the G-N, or the "separate–not separate," continuum is highly influenced by socioeconomic conditions. The people of Catalonia are much more liberal and affluent than the vulnerable both in the United States and in Europe, but their interests point in the national direction—and this is where they stand.

As economic interests are not evenly distributed even within small nations, disagreements are likely to occur within

Catalan election results 2017
Percentage of people voting for pro-independence parties

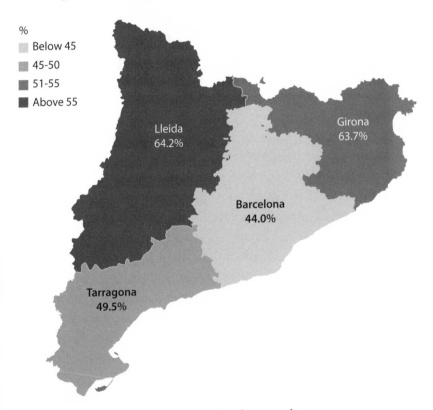

FIGURE 7. 2017 Catalan election results.
Source: Catalan government.

separatist regions. The map in Figure 7 showing the 2017 election results in Catalonia echoes other maps presented in this book, with the megacities (Barcelona in the Catalan case) being more heterogeneous, open to the world, and less enthusiastic about independence than the more homogenous and less prosperous interior lands that favor independence.

Why do Catalans want self-rule? Would they be as enthusiastic about it if they were less affluent? Is a desire to keep one's wealth at home enough to make one a nationalist? These questions demonstrate how difficult it is to separate national aspirations and economic interests. The mere fact that an economic demand marries itself to nationalism allows it to be heard, but does not automatically make it just. From the point of view of justice, the attempts of the vulnerable to use nationalism in order to re-create a cross-class coalition seem justified as much as the attempts to use it to re-create white supremacy are unwarranted. Similarly, the claims of the affluent for greater cultural and political autonomy are much more justified than their claims to be less generous to poorer regions. Are we having a debate about justice disguised as a national debate? The answer is yes! The growing social and economic gaps, alongside the democratic crisis, provoke a discussion about fundamental political questions: How are we to define the boundaries of political units and who is to be included within them? Nationalism provides an acceptable justification: first to the question of the boundaries issue, then to the definition of "the people," and finally to distributive issues. The alternative is to accept the arbitrariness of political (and personal) life, admitting that, when circumstances will change, other solutions may be viable or desirable. This is likely to invite short-termism, undermining the feeling of inevitability states rely on, assuring their citizens that this is our land, our country, our traditions, and these are the obligations that come with it.

Can separatists succeed despite the fact that their claims challenge the integrity of existing states? The sustainability of existing states is a powerful motivational force; hence, I allow myself to predict that in the foreseeable future the old nation-states are unlikely to fall apart, but within the European sphere two processes most probably would gather momentum: the strengthening of local cultures and languages (2018 has been declared the European Year of Cultural Heritage, celebrating the diversity of European cultures) and the erosion of state-based distributive systems, thus giving affluent regions (Catalonia, Flanders, Basque country) more control over their resources. This has already happened in Belgium, where the Flemish Party (the New Flemish Alliance) has given up the struggle for independence in return for undoing the shared social safety net, moving certain services, such as child allowance and health care, from the federal to the regional level. The Basque region gained control over its own tax receipts and the Catalans are also likely to compromise on a greater economic, cultural, and political autonomy that would allow them to better protect their assets in return for independence. Separatist nationalism is therefore leading in the opposite direction from the nationalism of the vulnerable—its end result is the erosion of civic solidarity and deeper social gaps. Although its language is inclusive and easier to endorse, separatism may be the less morally valuable of the two kinds of nationalism. Separatism aspirations are here to stay; their effect on future political events will be much less significant than those of the nationalism of the vulnerable—for once justice may have the upper hand.

Part IV

A New Social Contract

It's time to fight back, Nationalism can, and should be reclaimed for liberals.

YASCHA MOUNK, HOW LIBERALS CAN
RECLAIM NATIONALISM

The nations we are imagining aspire to justice. They want to figure out how emotions can help them in their work, motivating good policies and rendering them stable. They also want to thwart, or at least to control, emotions that would derail their efforts.

MARTHA NUSSBAUM, POLITICAL EMOTIONS:
WHY LOVE MATTERS FOR JUSTICE

19

Liberal Nationalism

Reaching the end of our journey, the bottom line is clear: though the nation-state's powers have been eroded, its solidarity worn, its distributive powers limited, and cultural homogeneity challenged, the theoretical inability to define an alternative set of agreed-on, applicable moral and political principles leaves the nation-state the only viable option. Despite internal and external pressures, it "has proven remarkably resilient and remains the main determinant of the global distribution of income, the primary locus of market-supporting institutions, and the chief repository of personal attachments and affiliation."[1]

Globalism failed to replace nationalism because it couldn't offer a political agenda that meets the most basic needs of modern individuals: the desire to be autonomous and self-governing agents, the will to live a meaningful life that stretches beyond the self, the need to belong, the desire to be part of a creative community, to feel special, find a place in the chain of being, and to enjoy a sense (or the illusion) of stability and cross-generational continuity.

Those who believed that postindustrial, postmodern societies would promote the development of new political structures grounded in a division of labor between different spheres of human life—economic globalism, local culturalism, and regional democracies—have a reason to be disappointed. The discussion of Nutopia explains why these kinds of solutions are too open and discontinuous to allow a welfare democracy to work. Two decades of hyperglobalism taught us four important lessons:

a. A divorce between markets and political systems works against the worst off, leaving them exposed to higher risks and fewer opportunities. It leads to growing social and economic gaps and allows the 1 percent to drift further and further away from the 99 percent. The middle classes, losing their social holding and social status, join the lower classes in nurturing a deep sense of social and economic pessimism. Society disintegrates, spreading a sense of alienation and anomie.

b. The distance between local, regional, and global decision-making processes deepens the democratic deficit. The growing power of mega global corporations and international institutions ridicules the democratic aspiration of individuals to be "the authors of their lives." Helplessness, pessimism, and social passivity spread.

c. Feelings of frustration and despair intensify political distrust and deepen social schisms. Society turns from a locus of cooperation into a battlefield.

d. The separation of culture and politics leaves cultures open to economic exploitation and states void of a creative mission.

In his book *If Venice Dies?*, Salvatore Settis[2] argues that cities die in different ways: they could be destroyed or captured by a powerful enemy or they could be taken captive by capitalism. The commercialization and globalization of cities means they are losing their souls, tempted to produce cheap replicas rather than original cultural products. Their inhabitants become foreigners in their own land, often choosing to go elsewhere. The city is emptied of permanent residences and falls prey to the momentary passions of passers-by. Similar processes happen to states that turn into faint replicas of what they used to be; no wonder there is a growing desire to bring back some of the normative, economic, political, and cultural values lost in the age of hyperglobalism.

Nationalism is called back as a content provider, but its return is far from innocent, it opens up a Pandora's box that hosts fears from the past as well as present-day anxieties. There are then no easy choices. Meaningful communities are, by their very nature, appealing to some and exclusionary for others. One the most important lessons of the present crisis is that inclusion, not exclusion, has its costs.

Heisenberg's uncertainty principle teaches us that we must sacrifice either the accuracy of measuring the momentum of a particle or its position. Similarly, we must acknowledge that either the meaningfulness and internal cohesiveness of community or its openness must be sacrificed as we cannot have them both. A cultural version of the Heisenberg uncertainty principle may suggest the following:

> One cannot create communities that are both meaningful and entirely open: the more meaningful a community is to its members the more exclusive it would be to all others.

Acknowledging that some sacrifices must be made in order to allow democratic states the ability to be politically and culturally engaging is an important political lesson. Ignoring it seems self-serving. As Ivan Krastev argues, the inability and the unwillingness of liberal elites to acknowledge and discuss the destabilizing force of diversity and migration and contend with their consequences, "and the insistence that existing policies are always positive sum (win-win), are what make liberalism for so much synonymous with hypocrisy."[3] The revolt against liberal idealism is fundamentally reshaping Europe's (as well as America's) political landscape.

Or maybe it's not hypocrisy but part of the liberal illusion, well grounded in the Enlightenment, that all good things go hand in hand. It is natural to wish that all valuable social processes will support each other, that pluralism and democracy will be reinforcing, openness and commitment will go hand in hand, while fairness and care will lead to the same social solutions. Unfortunately, that is not the case. Quite often they lead in conflicting directions. As a result we are forced to make difficult choices.

A common means of avoiding the moral conflicts raised by a clash of ideologies, of making nationalism more palatable and less threatening to liberals and democrats, is painting nationalism in a civic light, offering a nationalism that is free of all exclusionary aspects, grounded in citizenship and void of all exclusionary features. Is this kind of nationalism viable?

The longing for a civic nationalism that annuls the role of culture, language, religion, ethnicity, or race—and therefore never leads to exclusion or xenophobia—is understandable, but it has little to rely on. It takes us back to the early days of identity politics (the late 1980s) and forces us to revisit the complex interplay among politics, culture, and identity. In the first round, identity politics voiced the complaint of members of minority groups against the liberal vision of the neutral state. It forced the majority to acknowledge that cultural, national, and linguistic affiliations determine not only who we are but also what we get. Progressives became sympathetic to these arguments, and identity politics turned into a major ideological pillar of twenty-first-century liberalism. In order to remedy identity biases, minorities demanded the reshaping of the public sphere, making space for their own particular identities. Diversification became the liberal war cry.

Today, protests regarding the identity of the public sphere are raised again—this time by the less well-off members of the majority, claiming diversity went too far, ripping from them their social, cultural, and political status. The liberal response is dismissive. The dismissal of identity demands raised by members of the majority has more to it than just a refusal to allow the privileged to retain power—it reflects the disinterest of the elites in their own national identity.

An inclusive image of the public sphere paints it in an ideal light that wishes to make conflicts go away. Idealistic descriptions are dangerous as they can easily lead to misguided expectations and harmful policies. Worse still, presenting an ideal as a reflection of reality creates the impression that the desired change has already happened (or is happening) and fosters the illusion that nothing much needs to be done, or at least that things are under control, going the right way.

Here is one example of many: Emmanuel Macron, the French president, opened and closed his election campaign in Marseille, one of France's most diverse cities, with a mixed population of French-born residents and immigrants from all over the world. It was in Marseille that Macron chose to make his speech about Frenchness:

> When I look at Marseille, I see a French city, shaped by two thousand years of history, or immigration, of Europe . . . I see Armenians Italians, Algerians, Moroccans, Tunisians. I see so many people from Mali, from Senegal, from the Ivory Coast, I see so many others I haven't mentioned. But what do I see? I see the people of Marseille! What do I see? I see the people of France! Look at them. They are here. They are proud. Proud of being French. Take a good look at them. Ladies and Gentlemen of the *Front National*: this is what it means to be proud to be French.[4]

Reality, however, is quite different. The people of Marseille feel much less certain about their identity. Some of them openly share their pain. "It's difficult," says Mohammed, "to find a job if you have the wrong address or the wrong kind of name, such as anything Arabic." He cites a friend, a fully qualified engineer unable to get an interview: "If he puts Jean-Michel on his CV, it'd be a different story."[5]

Driving around Paris in one of the many neighborhoods inhabited by minorities, the picture becomes clearer. Bondy, the place where the new French football hero, Kylian Mbappé, grew up, is one of Paris's suburbs, a place inhabited by "working-class, nonwhite communities, synonymous with riots and social strife, thought of as breeding grounds for crime and terrorism."[6] Mbappé's neighbors are French, but like many other minority groups they feel less included in the French society than Macron would have liked us (and them) to believe. Urban segregation has worsened in France in recent decades; the social stratification of residential districts determines access to quality education and subsequently further upward social mobility for the individuals who live there. This residential segregation has a clear ethnic dimension. "In some urban districts, relations can only be governed by violence, and those living there cannot experience upward social mobility. They wonder what integration means. The fact of cohabiting with residents of a poor neighborhood and sharing their social problems leads them to social behaviors that are too different from those of the middle classes or society 'as a whole.'"[7] The overlap of poverty, ethnicity, and estrangement intensifies social schisms and helps paint immigrants in a nonfavorable light. The poor are left to struggle among themselves as to who is offending whom, while the well-off, secluded in their protected neighborhoods, are busy explaining to them that they are all equal.

This is not only a French or an American challenge; the situation in most Western countries is similar. The lack of structural policies of integration and accommodation, decades of failures, misunderstandings, and missed opportunities, and "a recurring and stubborn tendency to ignore reality," led to the present volatile situation.[8] In Germany, for millions of Turkish immigrants (many of whom are second- and third-generation), integration is more of an aspiration than reality. The slow process of accommodation is grounded in the initial assumption that the "guest workers" will return to their homeland. The 1961 labor-recruitment agreement between West Germany and Turkey was therefore discussed in economic rather than cultural terms. Eager to recruit young Turks at the prime of their labor capacity, Germany succumbed to demands to bring semiskilled or unskilled poorly paid workers to take over unpopular jobs and supported immigration from poor and remote regions of Turkey. The guest workers were expected to live near the factories and return to Turkey after working for a few years. Hence, "no one in Germany cared much about the fact that many of the new arrivals could hardly read or write, making it difficult for them to participate in German society."[9]

Mounting pressures from German industries, which didn't want to go through the burden of recruiting and training new workers, led to the removal of the "rotation clause," intended to limit a foreign worker's initial stay in Germany to two years. Realizing that they were not going back, workers settled in cheap neighborhoods, leading to the rise of immigrant neighborhoods that now are seen as the strongholds of so-called parallel societies. Germany is now paying the price of the ongoing avoidance of dealing with challenges of integration and the social effects of the growing cultural tensions.

Even in Sweden, one of the most open social democracies, the extreme right is becoming stronger. For decades, Sweden was a racially and culturally homogeneous country with an expansive social welfare system. Swedes insisted that they could absorb large numbers of non-European migrants, but they never asked themselves how those migrants would be integrated into Swedish society.

In other cities across Western Europe, migrants tended to cluster in low-income neighborhoods; facing poor job prospects and rampant employment discrimination, they naturally turned inward. More young women have started wearing the hijab recently, Mr. Abdirahman says, and more young men "internalize the otherness"—rejected by their new society, they embrace the stereotypes imposed on them.[10] This allowed the extreme right-wing party, Sweden Democrats, to solicit growing support that is going to change the Swedish political landscape.

When Angela Merkel says that Islam is part of Germany, claiming that "we are all Germany," and when Macron looks at the people of Marseilles, saying "this is France," they nurture the illusion that national affiliations, culture, language, tradition, and religion do not matter. Not only is this description imprecise, but it also leaves the "left behind" to fight each other for goods that are not valued by the elites yet are necessary for their survival.

In his book *The People vs. Democracy*, Yascha Mounk[11] acknowledges the return of nationalism and argues that it should be domesticated. The future, he argues, demands that we shall build on a tradition of multiethnic democracy "to show that the ties that bind us go well beyond ethnicity and religion." Is there really such a tradition? Multiethnic empires and monarchies— yes; a multiethnic commonwealth—indeed, but multicultural, multiethnic democracies have a very poor track record.

Liberals like to believe that social diversity breeds tolerance and open-mindedness, but research does not support this. Even in the United States, diversity intensifies the spread of native sentiments and harsh laws on immigration.[12] As Carol Larsen's comparative study shows, growing multiculturalism pushes even the most liberal countries closer to the national pole.[13] When asked in 1995 about aspects defining their identity, 52 percent of Canadians emphasized being born in the country, 55 percent stressed living most of one's life in Canada, and 26 percent highlighted being Christian. When asked the same question in 2003, after two decades of growing diversity, the national point of view was reinforced: 82 percent emphasized being born in the country, and 83 percent and 54 percent, respectively, emphasized living most of one's life in Canada and being Christian.[14] Contrary to many predictions, extensive diversity evoked a growing emphasis on birthrights rather than choice. The reason is clear—diversity was never a goal—it was a compromise based on the assumption that the social reality is stable and unlikely to change. The acceptance of diversity, hence, piggybacked on a sense of security. When cultural and political identity was cemented and nationalism turned banal, giving room to a wider range of social, cultural, ethnic, racial, and linguistic representations seemed harmless. In this stage of "assumed stability," the nation-state could easily take pride in its ability to accommodate internal differences, congratulating itself on outgrowing "national infancy" and maturing into a civic stage.

At a certain point the transformation of the public sphere turned from stimulating and invigorating into threatening. When the threshold of "reasonable diversity" is crossed, social cohesion collapses and the balance of power is tilted back in the direction of homogenization. The majority, especially its most vulnerable members, realizes the influence of this process on its ability to cash its national capital and starts worrying about the disintegration of the familiar social fabric. Fearing the loss of status and opportunities and being exposed to a greater internal and external competition, vulnerable members of the majority become more defensive, trying to reclaim some of the traditional structures of the nation-state.

This process is accelerated in times of austerity. When social resources are scarce, the ideological wind changes and more nationalistic voices settle in, reflecting an anti-diversity and anti-immigration mood and a desire to revive some of the policies effective in the first stages of nation-building. Experiments, Krastev argues, have demonstrated that "people are far readier to tolerate migrants not only when they judge their numbers acceptable but also when they see signs of their successful integration."[15] In other words, people rightly wish that social changes will be moderated and managed.

While states neglected the role of planning and monitoring integration and accommodation, the market determined both the number of immigrants and the spread of the costs and benefits of their inclusion. Like in so many other cases, this means that those who benefit and those who carry the burden are two separate groups. The benefits go to those who use the cheap labor and profit from it, and the burdens are placed on the shoulders of the less well-off members of the society who are struggling to keep their jobs, protect the value of their property, and maintain the quality of their schools. Ignoring this injustice was/is a fatal political and moral mistake.

Rather than asking who is for or against diversity, maybe it's time to stop and think not in *for* and *against* terms but in terms of degrees: how much diversity can be taken in while retaining social cohesion? How fast can a society adjust to demographic changes? Who carries the burden of such changes, and can these be more evenly distributed? The mere fact of asking these questions could sow the seeds of a new discourse that does not position people against one another but tries to offer applicable solutions.

In searching for a proper solution it is important to remember that the current social and political unrest is grounded not only in an economic crisis but also in a crisis of identity for which the civic version of nationalism offers an insufficient, too abstract and legalistic answer. Constitutionalism, universal rights, and equal membership are valuable guidelines for political action, but they cover a limited scope of a person's life. Most of all, they offer a very thin base for social and political cooperation. This is why nationalism keeps coming back, pushing civic ideals aside, making its way to center stage. Those who will know how to espouse it will be the winners of the coming decades.

20

This Is the Time

National sentiments, I argue, should be used to induce a readiness to rebuild a cross-class coalition, giving individuals worthwhile reasons to work together to promote the common good, securing a more just distribution of risks and opportunities. There are four reasons why this is the right time to do so:

First, as we have already seen, processes of globalization have deepened the rift between the privileged globetrotter elite and the many bound to stay home. More and more residents of the developed world realize that they are far more rooted in their homelands than globalists would have liked to believe. Realizing that their personal fate is tied with that of their country, it is only logical for them to wish to put it first.

Second, understanding that the era of Western domination is coming to an end and that power is being redistributed across the globe in new and unknown ways instills fear and places many in the developed world on the side of the vulnerable. The shift in global hegemony forces democracies to explore new ways of defending their citizens' long-term interests. Hyperglobalism united the "99 percent," class structure became fluid, and a growing percentage of the middle class felt increasingly insecure and exposed to the risks of the less well-off. Thus a cross-class coalition seems more attractive than ever, and with it emerges the demand to bring the elites back home, convincing (even forcing) them to share their wealth with fellow nationals.

Third, some of the traditional social tools used to promote greater social cohesion are not working as well as they used to. It was commonly assumed that in the twenty-first century— when so many jobs require advanced human skills—better education is the key for greater competitiveness. Nowadays, in the developed world, more and more people realize that education is not enough to secure a prosperous life. State intervention is necessary in order to build an infrastructure that will allow the educated to make good use of their skills, investing in research and development, in the preservation of jobs as well as in the creation of new ones. The days of the lean, minimal state, when it was enough to nurture skills and then practice noninterference in order to protect the ability of citizens to make the best use of their accumulated human capital are over. Nowadays, state planning, financing, and monitoring are necessary preconditions for providing citizens with good enough opportunities while minimizing their risks.

Fourth, the need for planning is especially urgent in light of the crisis of the millennials who, in the developed world, had a run of bad luck:

> Capital losses in the global financial crisis of 2008–2009 and high subsequent unemployment have dealt serious blows to young workers and savers. Add rising student debt in several developed countries, tighter mortgage rules after 2008, higher house prices, increased income inequality, less access to pensions and lower income mobility and you have a "perfect storm" holding back wealth accumulation by the Millennials in many countries.[1]

As a result, the millennials are likely to experience greater challenges and greater wealth inequality than those in previous generations. State-directed actions must be taken in order to allow them to conduct a productive and satisfying life. Nothing threatens democratic stability more than unmet expectations and unused skills. Invisible hands cannot draw and protect borders, distribute resources, create jobs, foster solidarity and social empathy, or motivate tolerance and accommodation. The state needs to renter the public and economic sphere in order to make a difference.

If the new task of the state is to reestablish a cross-class coalition that will promote a fairer distribution of risks and opportunities, it is important to acknowledge that some risks and opportunities are unifying—promoting social cohesiveness and undermining class tensions—while others are divisive—pulling the different classes in different directions and exacerbating social conflict. Unfortunately, the social and economic costs and benefits of unifying risks such as war or social conflict are easier to imagine than the costs and benefits of unifying opportunities and goods. The destruction caused by the former and the social unity that follows is evident, whereas the benefits of the latter are quite obscure as they often reflect the avoidance of disruptive events such as social crisis, growing gaps, strikes, riots, or even revolution. Consequently, when seeking unity, individuals are less motivated to invest in risk prevention than in conflict promotion, hence the close affinity between internal crisis and belligerent policies. Social crisis and intolerance are therefore common bedfellows.

Opportunities can also be unifying or divisive. They are unifying when they are open to everyone and distributed in ways that serve the common good; they are divisive when they are unequally or unfairly allocated, or, worse still, open to only a select few. The divisive effect of opportunities is well exemplified by the nationalism of the vulnerable. A common theme among the vulnerable is that they were twice betrayed: once when the state did not prevent the dwindling of their opportunities, and twice when it willingly handed over the few opportunities created to those who "jumped the line."

The line jumpers—women, blacks, immigrants, and indigenous people who were found to be deserving of affirmative action—gained new opportunities while the vulnerable were left behind. The individualization of poverty and the unmaking of class-based policies placed poor members of the majority in a disadvantaged position—having fewer opportunities and of a lesser quality. No wonder many of them conclude that the state is unsympathetic to their needs, taking the side of "the others."[2] When those who need the state the most do not trust its intentions, they are tempted to join anarchist, populist, and antiliberal forces that offer no solution but adequately express their rage.

The situation gets even more volatile when it becomes clear that it's not only opportunities that are unevenly distributed but also the costs of collective risks: those who pay the highest price for policies such as free trade, free movements of people, and affirmative action are those who rejected these policies, while those advocating them avoid carrying their burden. The uneven distribution of risks and opportunities explains the felt injustice and consequently the aggression associated with the nationalism of the vulnerable.

Resistance to social change may be an innate attitude, but it is intensified by feelings of unfairness. An ongoing neglect of the obligation to compensate, support, and bail out individuals who went bankrupt, while going all the way to support banks and investment companies on the verge of collapse, made the distorted political order of priorities clear. A targeted attempt to redistribute costs and benefits in a more just and effective way could ameliorate negative feelings, promote a greater sense of

TABLE 1. The social role of risks and opportunities

Risk	Opportunity	
Collective risks: war, terrorism, ecological risks, natural disasters. Welfare policies sharing risks in a fair way across the community.	Collective goods: National goods. Goods that are collectively produced and consumed, distributed in ways allowing all participants to win some gains.	**Unifying**
Selective risks to which only some members of the society are exposed. Uneven distribution of burdens.	Zero-sum goods. Goods only some can enjoy. Unequal distribution of goods that leaves some members of the society permanently on the losing side.	**Divisive**

fairness, reduce social tensions, and promote a readiness to re-build a cross-class cooperation.

In order to develop and implement policies that foster justice and fairness, one must convince the more powerful members of society that compromising their privileges and sharing their wealth and power is worth their while. No social and economic change can happen if the haves are not ready to level-down their power, wealth, and expectations. Some of the very wealthy members of society, individuals like Warren Buffet and Bill Gates, already declared their intention to contribute most of their fortune to promote social well-being. This is not enough—charity is an honorable act, yet it leaves the haves in control of the have-nots. What is needed is building social safety nets grounded in rights rather than empathy.

The present social task is looking inwardly, shifting the social and economic balance in ways that will allow a more even distribution of risks and opportunities. Such moves are likely to make a difference, yet the most important tool is a moral one. Making globalism the selfish choice and nationalism the moral one, moving the weight of justice from defending free trade and free movement to fighting poverty and closing social and economic gaps can change the basic perceptions of public morality. Most people wish to legitimize their actions and feel uneasy about supporting immoral, antisocial policies; pulling the moral and ideological rug from under hyperglobalism, forcing people to think twice before they turn their backs on their own fellow nationals, may be the beginning of a significant social and political change.

21

A Race to the Bottom

THE NEW SOCIAL CONTRACT

Making a difference, countering feelings of hostility and fear while reducing felt injustice by offering a fairer and more just political order, requires trusting the state, supporting social planning, and cementing the basis of a new social contract that sets out innovative ways of redistributing risks and opportunities. No wonder Franklin Delano Roosevelt's name is up in the air. He had, Mark Lilla asserts, a vision of "what we were as citizens, what was owed to us, what we owed to each other. It was a political vision that legitimized the use of government to construct social solidarity and defend equal rights."[1] Roosevelt believed that the war had put class envy on the back burner "but had not solved the problem of creating emotional solidarity around economic issues."[2] Hence, he devoted a great deal of time and thought to the emotional underpinnings of social solidarity. The programs of the New Deal demanded sacrifices, and Roosevelt was out there convincing the public that they must shoulder the burden. He inspired people to adopt a political discourse that would reduce the role of hostile envy. He managed to ignite "a spirit of civic friendship and common work, convincing the disadvantaged that the nation will support their aspirations and attempting to convince the advantaged that narrow self-interest is un-American."[3] This last sentence defines the present task in the clearest possible way: asking the haves to look beyond their immediate interests must be justified not only in universal utilitarian terms but also as the national (American, Israeli, French) thing to do.

Nurturing "committed nationalism"—the nationalism of mutual responsibility that places fellow nationals at the top of one's social priorities—may help to rebuild social solidarity. Basing such responsibilities on things we have in common—norms, traditions, ways of life and habits of the heart, a common past, and a desire for a better future—will tighten the social fabric and make it more resilient. And though there would certainly be disagreements about how to define the American, French, or Israeli thing to do, turning our eyes inwardly is, in and of itself, a massive step forward as it will allow us to see things that for decades have been veiled.

If such changes happen, the state will become more trustworthy. Presently we are caught in a vicious circle: trust eludes us when we need it the most. "The extent to which citizens perceive themselves and their families to be economically insecure has a statistically significant and substantial negative effect on political trust."[4] Hence, the deeper the economic crisis gets: felt injustice exacerbates, political trust declines, and public satisfaction with the way democracy functions is lessened.[5] It is therefore not surprising that among millennials, support for democracy is plummeting; a growing percentage believe it is not the best way to govern and would prefer a strong leader free of constraints. There is no easy way out of this circle, yet convincing citizens that they can do no better than trust the state they fear is necessary for moving ahead and changing the rules of the game.

The understanding that the nation-state in its full political, cultural, and communal capacity, must be brought back into play is growing. You know this is the order of the day when political leaders from both sides of the isle are calling to place national affiliations before global ones. Bernie Sanders says to American billionaires, "you cannot continue to take advantage of all the benefits of America, if you refuse to accept your responsibilities,"[6] while on the other side of the Atlantic and the other pole of the political spectrum, Theresa May repeats the same line of argument:

> Today, too many people in positions of power behave as though they have more in common with international elites than with the people down the road, the people they employ, the people they pass in the street. But if you believe you're a citizen of the world, you're a citizen of nowhere. You don't understand what the very word "citizenship" means. Just listen to the way a lot of politicians and commentators talk about the public. They find your patriotism distasteful, your concerns about immigration parochial, your views about crime illiberal, your attachment to your job security inconvenient. They find the fact that more than seventeen million voters decided to leave the European Union simply bewildering.[7]

It is interesting to see how conservatives and social democrats now rally around the nation-state, looking to bring the elites back home in the name of both nationalism and social justice. This alliance isolates liberals who keep preaching to the people that they have got it wrong, that things are going all right. Rather than listening and seeking ways to make people feel safer, liberal elites try to make them feel blameworthy (or simply stupid). But the vulnerable would like to see action first and apologies later.

The affinity between right and left is such that it is often difficult to guess if a text was written by a conservative or a social democrat. Here is one example:

I'm in this to stand up for the weak and stand up to the strong, to put the power of government squarely at the service of ordinary working-class people. . . . It's easy to say that all you want from government is for it to get out of the way. But a change has got to come. It's time to remember the good that government can do. Time for a new approach that says while government does not have all the answers, government can and should be a force for good; that the state exists to provide what individual people, communities and markets cannot; and that we should employ the power of government for the good of the people.[8]

This is Theresa May, but it could have been Bernie Sanders, Jeremy Corbin (her worst political rival), Elizabeth Warren, or even the new radical Democratic candidate from New York, Alexandria Ocasio-Cortez. Ocasio-Cortez identifies herself as a working-class New Yorker who experienced, along with her peers, the mounting social challenges of the last twenty years, when life got harder and less secure. She shatters the optimistic picture of progress painted by public figures such as President Obama or Michael Moore. For her this is not the best of times. She acknowledges that things have gone wrong and that some of her party's leaders have crossed the class line and collaborated with the powerful against the worse off.

Ocasio-Cortez is therefore eager to draw a distance between herself and other Democrats. "It's time we acknowledged that not all Democrats are the same. That a Democrat who takes corporate money, profits off foreclosure, doesn't live here, doesn't send his kids to our schools, doesn't drink our water or breathe our air cannot possibly represent us."[9]

A more centrist Democrat, Elizabeth Warren, is also eager to distance herself from corporate Democrats promoting the "accountable capitalism act" meant to address an epidemic of bad corporate behavior, "especially the tendency of top executives to value profits over wider well-being. It would obligate executives to consider the interests of all corporate stakeholders—including employees, customers and communities—not just shareholders and would require that at least 40 percent of company board members be elected by employees, an idea known as co-determination."[10]

Social policies likes Medicare for all, a living wage, free tuition for public colleges, a federal jobs guarantee, greater intervention and regulations of corporate management, and closure of tax havens are going to become the order of the day. Right and left, Republicans and Democrats, conservatives and progressives will all try to convince the lower classes to trust them (and the state) in order to form a new cross-class coalition, rebuilding bridges among all fellow nationals.

It is no surprise that the emergence of social democratic policies and national feelings go hand in hand. As I have argued, one cannot advocate at the same time both open borders and a generous welfare system. Nevertheless, the close affinity between welfare policies and political closure was often ignored; consequently, both progressives and conservative are surprised to find out that while they preach for the one they may end up with the other. Britain is a poignant example: Leaving the European Union, a fantasy of Thatcherites who wanted to turn Britain into a European version of Singapore, has been redefined as a way of boosting spending on health and limiting immigration—"taking back control" rather than "letting the market rip."[11] In Britain the frontiers of the state are rolling forward as privatized services are taken over by the state. "Britain's leftward drift can be seen in one opinion poll after another. A survey published by Legatum in 2017 found that 83% of Britons favored public ownership of water, 77% of electricity and gas, and 76% of railways."[12] French president Immanuel Macron now advocates state patriotism, endorsing policies that include a wide range of solutions to the weakening safety net from pension reforms to workers' training and lifelong learning. Not surprisingly these coincide with stricter control on foreign investments, protection of local investors, and new tariffs and taxes, are meant to allow France to actively defend its citizens.

The political balance thus tilts in the direction of the nationalism of the vulnerable rather than in the direction of the nationalism of the affluent. This is no coincidence, although the vulnerable associate themselves all too often with murky partners; they are presenting morally justified social and political claims. Fighting extremism and a sense of supremacy on the one hand, while attending to the real needs of the vulnerable on the other, will make political systems more caring and just.

A political avalanche has started rolling down the hill; on the way, it will erode soil and shake rocks exposing new groups where new theories could flourish. It might end very far from where it started. What started as a conservative rebellion against liberal progressive elites ends up restructuring the ideological map. The new political map will be arranged along two dimensions: the first, as Ocasio-Cortez blatantly defines it, "the People vs. Money," the mobile against the immobile, the 99 percent against the 1 percent. The other is the state against the free market. Neoglobalism has forced the people and the state to one pole and the 1 percent and neoliberalism to the other, and the democratic outcomes are quite predictable.

The buzzwords of the twentieth century—small governments, neutral public spheres, free markets, free trade, and free movement—are in the process of being replaced by national affiliations, economic patriotism, and social responsibility. According to Robert Reich, the real choice ahead is between oligarchy and state patriotism based on what we owe each other. Bernie Sanders seconds: "The major issue of our time is the rapid movement toward international oligarchy in which a handful of billionaires own and control a significant part of the global economy." This suggests that the globalism-nationalism continuum is in the process of being replaced with a new one that stretches between world oligarchy and state patriotism. These new definitions are very telling: globalism is easy to endorse; world oligarchy is easy to reject. It is not difficult to guess in which direction the political pendulum is moving.

As we enter the age of a new and caring nationalism, a warning should be aired. National partnerships that are profitable to some are dangerous to others. There is no solidarity without in-group favoritism, stereotyping, and other negative side effects of group membership. Nationalism can be tamed, but it cannot be constructed in ways that run counter to human nature and social psychology. The hope to have patriotism without flags, hymns, and symbols and a sense of identity that by its very nature is inclusive contradicts everything we know about the way groups are formed. Four moves must therefore be taken to tame the new nationalism and make it more liberal and tolerant.

First, the demand to put one's country first should not be grounded in a sense of superiority but in a belief that others have the same right (and duty) to pursue their goals. This universal view of national affiliations would allow individuals to defend their rights while respecting other peoples' national commitments. This kind of liberal nationalism, grounded in universal national rights, does not turn its back on the world but uses national entities as a springboard from which one can leap to a world better governed.[13]

This approach demands that nation-states will reengage in nation building, as none could flourish without social, cultural, and political investment. Nation-states around the world must be engaged in defining their collective credo. This is not a call for political unanimity but an understanding that national affiliations are grounded in culture, language, political principles, traditions, and history or religion, and they must spell out these uniting features and make them evident by means of education and public discourse. This also is not a conservative call to discourage change, but a cautious progressive call to plan, manage, and administrate social changes in order to prevent unintentional destructive results.

Some may fear that an attempt to form and disseminate a shared conception of the public good calls for a far too pervasive state intervention. This indeed could be the case if taken to the extreme. Yet on the other side of the equation lie the dangers embedded in cultural destruction, social anarchy, and democratic downfall. Like every other idea presented in this book, the new wave of nation building should be balanced against other values, but states must have a raison d'être. If we want democracies to survive they must have a meaning that goes beyond utilitarianism; they should therefore seek nationalism's supportive hand.

Second, as no country is culturally, ethnically, or religiously homogenous, the place of minorities must be secured. The fact that they do not share the ruling national ethos, culture, or language should not be used against them. Respect for the rights and choices of others should be consolidated internally as much as it is respected internationally. Meeting the social, economic, and cultural needs of the vulnerable without cultivating fear and hatred is necessary if we are seeking new solutions rather than new victims.

The nurturing of national identity should thus be complemented with actively fostering empathy for citizens who are not fellow nationals. Emphasizing the role of the state as a homeland ought to reinforce rather than negate the state's contractual basis and the benefits that come with it. Indigenous people, minorities, immigrants, or foreigners all have a right to be defended and respected. Unlike civic nationalism, liberal nationalism does not ignore the role of identity and membership; hence, it is inherently attentive to (rather than dismissive of) the disadvantages associated with being a minority and seeks sways of ameliorating them.

Third, the desire to reduce animosity and allow the different social classes and national groups to live together despite inevitable tensions demands that all citizens feel they are fairly treated. Felt injustice is one of the strongest motivations for social violence. Consequently, social risks and opportunities must be distributed in just and transparent ways. Most important of all, the less well-off should not be forced to carry an unfair share of the social burdens and risks. Whatever policies are agreed on and adopted—from a generous immigration policy to changing the structure of the economy—the resulting burdens and benefits should be distributed in ways that empower the weak and restrain the power of the privileged.

Last but not least, it is important to revive a sense of social and political optimism and collective pride that allows individuals and societies to envision a better future for themselves and for the coming generations. Nothing makes a society more brutal than a sense of despair that cannot be mitigated.

What I am therefore suggesting is to rebuild societies on the basis of a mélange of values and ideas borrowing from different schools of thought in order to create an untidy but decent and workable compromise. Such a compromise may not fit the aspirations of theoreticians, yet it reflects the complexity of human nature and of social life. The ideological modesty advocated earlier alongside a combination of realism and idealism may produce the necessary cure.

To realize the relative validity of one's convictions, Isaiah Berlin argued, and yet to stand for them unflinchingly is what distinguishes a civilized man from a barbarian: "To demand more than this is perhaps a deep and incurable metaphysical need; but to allow it to determine one's practice is a symptom of an equally deep, and more dangerous, moral and political immaturity."[14]

Our responsibility is to act in a well-balanced way. Whenever asked how much of each value we should pour into our ideological hodgepodge, Berlin would say: "just the right amount." He believed it was our moral and civic duty to make our own judgments. As there is no one, true answer that could be revealed in a moment of enlightenment rooted in either pure reason or religious revelation, it is for humans to think and act. With no recipe book to describe how a good society should be constructed, it is up to us to make our society better. This is why freedom is essential for those constantly seeking bearable and livable compromises.

Each idea presented in this book could and has been taken to the extreme. Compromises and middle-of-the-road solutions are less common and not very popular these days. The emergence of extreme forms of nationalism, affiliated with xenophobia, racism, misogyny, and anti-Semitism, shows how easy it is to cross moral lines. But the dominance of neoliberal hyperglobalism and the injustice it creates show that too. The fact that both brutal neoliberalism and xenophobic nationalism have pushed us to the edge means that both should be restrained and balanced, their inner values adjusted and reshaped to meet the needs of the twenty-first century.

It would be a tragedy if nationalism—with its tremendous creative and productive powers—were left in the hands of extremists. Open-minded liberal democrats, social democrats, and justice-seeking individuals must learn to harness nationalism to their cause, creating a more just social order, closing socio-economic gaps, while providing people with a cultural and normative reference to live by.

The gloomy future many predict we are heading toward may actually be a beginning of a much-needed correction that will make it the best of times for many more individuals than just a thin privileged elite. Nationalism is a too powerful and flexible tool to be given up; it should be endorsed and reshaped to fit the needs of the coming generations. It would be no exaggeration to say that the political stability of modern democracies depends on the emergence of such a new equilibrium that makes room for care, loyalty, and belonging on the one hand while taming ethnocentrism and xenophobia on the other. The swing from neoliberal hyperglobalism to extreme right-wing nationalism is a devastating one. The biggest challenge of the century is to stop the ideological pendulum half way, offering a social contract that balances human rights and freedom with social solidarity and group identity. Historically, the right balance has rarely been found, but there is no task more important than its pursuit.

Notes

A Personal Note

1. Yuli (Yael) Tamir, "Class and Nation," in *Cultural Diversity versus Economic Solidarity: Is There a Tension? How Must It Be Resolved?*, ed. Phillippe Van Parijs (Brussels: Deboeck Universite, Francqui, Scientific Library, 2004), 152, 154.

Chapter 1: The New Nationalism

1. Michael Moore, "5 Reasons Why Trump Will Win," *Michael Moore*, https://michaelmoore.com/trumpwillwin/.

2. One should emphasize the fact that this book traces processes in the developed world. I am well aware of the fact that different processes happen in other parts of the world, and I make no attempt to analyze them as they are far beyond my expertise.

3. I borrow this concept from the excellent work of Dani Rodrik. See Dani Rodrik, *The Globalization Paradox* (Oxford: Oxford University Press, 2011).

4. Thomas Nagel, "Moral Lack," in *Mortal Questions* (Cambridge: Cambridge University Press, 1979), 34.

5. I am looking at nationalism in the West. Different processes happen in other regions of the world. For an excellent analysis of developments in India, see Maya Tudor, *The Promise of Power: The Origins of Democracy in India and Autocracy in Pakistan* (Cambridge: Cambridge University Press), 2013.

Chapter 2: Never Say Never

1. Erich Maria Remarque, *All Quiet on the Western Front* (New York: Picador, 1993), 192.

2. Ian Buruma, *Year Zero: A History of 1945* (London: Atlantic Books, 2013), 337.

3. Between 1945 and 1949 eleven new states were established: Vietnam, Indonesia, and Korea (north and south) (1945), Syria (1946), India and Pakistan (1947), Burma, Sri-Lanka, and Israel (1948), and Bhutan (1949).

4. Alvin Powell, "How Sputnik Changed U.S. Education," *Harvard Gazette*, October 11, 2007.

5. Jaromír Navrátil, ed., *The Prague Spring 1968: A National Security Archive Documents Reader* (New York: Central European University Press, 1998), 288–89.

6. Francis Fukuyama, "The End of History?," *National Interest* 16 (Summer 1989): 3–18, at 17 (PDF).

7. Fukuyama, "End of History?," 1.

8. Fukuyama, "End of History?," 1.

9. Lucy Prebble, *Enron* (London: Methuen Drama, 2009), 113–14.

10. Jongsoo Lee and Hyunsun Yoon, "Narratives of the Nation in the Olympic Opening Ceremonies: Comparative Analysis of Beijing 2008 and London 2012," *Nations and Nationalism* 23, no. 4 (2017).

Chapter 3: Untidy Compromises

1. Michael Freeden, *Ideologies and Political Theory* (New York: Oxford University Press, 1998).

2. In my book *Liberal Nationalism* (Princeton, NJ: Princeton University Press, 1995), I highlight the similarities between these competing ideologies, arguing that we should find a way to include some of their fundamental values even at the price of some theoretical inconsistencies.

3. Isaiah Berlin, *Four Essays on Liberty* (New York: Oxford University Press, 1969), 39–40.

4. John Rawls, *A Theory of Justice* (Cambridge, MA: Harvard University Press, 1972), 137.

5. Joseph E. Stiglitz, *The Price of Inequality: How Today's Divided Society Endangers Our Future* (New York: Norton, 2012), 186.

Chapter 4: The Two Faces of Janus

1. Karl Popper, *The Open Society and Its Enemies*, vol. 2, 4th rev. ed. (London: Routledge and Kegan Paul, 1962), 49.

2. Mark Lilla, *The Shipwrecked Mind: On Political Reaction* (New York: New York Review of Books, 2016), xiii.

3. Eric J. Hobsbawm, *Nations and Nationalism since 1780: Program, Myth, Reality* (Cambridge: Cambridge University Press, 1999), 14.

4. Hobsbawm, *Nations and Nationalism*, 41.

5. Ernest Gellner, *Nations and Nationalism* (Oxford: Blackwell, 1983), 48.

6. Gellner, *Nations and Nationalism*, 22.

7. Liah Greenfeld, *Nationalism: Five Roads to Modernity* (Cambridge, MA: Harvard University Press, 1992), 18.

8. Cas Mudde, "Why Nativism, Not Populism, Should Be Declared Word of the Year," *The Guardian*, December 7, 2017.

9. Jan-Werner Müller, *What Is Populism?* (Philadelphia: University of Pennsylvania Press, 2016), 8.

10. Müller, *What Is Populism?*.

11. Müller, *What Is Populism?*.

12. Mudde, "Why Nativism, Not Populism."

13. Martha Nussbaum, *Political Emotions: Why Love Matters for Justice* (Cambridge, MA: Harvard University Press, 2013), 17.

14. Uri Pasovsky, "Prof. Dani Rodrik Declares: Leftists, It's Time to Be Patriots," *Calcalist*, August 3, 2017 (Hebrew).

Chapter 5: Nutopia

1. David Miller, *On Nationality* (Oxford: Oxford University Press, 1995), 24.

2. Liah Greenfeld, *Nationalism: Five Roads to Modernity* (Cambridge, MA: Harvard University Press, 1992), 10.

3. Canadian Council of Refugees, 2017 immigration level.

4. Benjamin Barber, "Liberal Democracy and the Cost of Consent," in *Liberalism and the Moral Life*, ed. Nancy Rosenblum (Cambridge, MA: Harvard University Press, 1989), 67.

5. Margaret Canovan, *Nationhood and Political Theory* (Cheltenham, England: Elgar, 1996), 69.

Chapter 6: Living beyond Our Psychological Means

1. Isaiah Berlin, *The Crooked Timber of Humanity*, 2nd ed. (London: Pimlico Press, 2013), 173.

2. The most important texts on this are to be found in Charles Taylor's two volumes, *Human Agency and Language* and *Philosophy and the Human Sciences* (Cambridge: Cambridge University Press, 1985).

3. In a religious or authoritarian culture this process of internalization is of lesser importance, as one is expected to follow orders or commands; not so in the modern world where personal autonomy is a virtue.

4. Will Kymlicka, *Liberalism, Community, and Culture* (Oxford: Oxford University Press, 1989), 192–93.

5. Charles Taylor, *The Ethics of Authenticity* (Cambridge, MA: Harvard University Press, 1991), 40–41.

6. Isaiah Berlin, "Benjamin Disraeli, Karl Marx, and the Search for Identity," in *Against the Current* (London: Hogarth Press, 1980), 255.

7. Isaiah Berlin, "Two Concepts of Liberty," in *Four Essays on Liberty* (Oxford: Oxford University Press, 1969), 156–57.

8. Berlin, "Two Concepts of Liberty," 157.

9. Roger Brown, *Social Psychology* (New York: Free Press, 1986), 541.

10. Michael A. Hogg and Dominic Abrams, "Social Motivation, Self-Esteem, and Social Identity," in *Social Identity Theory: Constructive and Critical Advances*, ed. D. Abrams and M. A. Hogg (New York: Harvester Wheatsheaf, 1990), 28–29.

11. Sigmund Freud, "Why War?," in *Character and Culture* (New York: Norton, 1971), 145.

12. Sigmund Freud, "Thoughts for Times of War and Death," in *Character and Culture*, 117.

13. Cited in George Kateb, "Notes on Pluralism," *Social Research* 61 (1994): 8.

14. David Miller, *On Nationality* (Oxford: Oxford University Press, 1995), 31.

15. Roger Brown, *Social Psychology* (New York: Free Press, 1965), 574.

16. W. G. Austin, "Justice in Intergroup Conflict," in *Psychology of Intergroup Relations*, ed. S. Worchel and W. A. Austin (Chicago: Nelson-Hall, 1986), 153.

17. For a brief description of the experiment see Brown, *Social Psychology*, 535–39.

18. Brown, *Social Psychology*, 533.

Chapter 7: Nation Building

1. Christine Emba, "Liberalism Is Loneliness," a review of *Why Liberalism Failed* by Patrick Deneen, *Washington Post*, April 6, 2018.

2. Michael Winerip, "The New Man and the Me Decade," *New York Times*, September 21, 2012.

3. Winerip, "New Man and the Me Decade."

4. Other ways of thinking, especially religious ones, can also play the role of a particular content provider, but their discourse is much more dangerous as it drives us away from the political sphere to the realm of the divine. Debates with holders of religious beliefs are very difficult to settle as their basic set of presuppositions is grounded in a different rationality that considers a mix of advantages that calculates benefits in the realms of life and afterlife. For further clarification of this complex issue see Yuli Tamir, "Remember Amalek, Religious Hate Speech," in *Obligations of Citizenship and Demands of Death*, ed. Nancy Rosenblum (Princeton, NJ: Princeton University Press, 2000); and Michael Walzer, *The Paradox of Liberation: Secular Revolution and Religious Counterrevolutions* (New Haven, CT: Yale University Press, 2015).

5. Anthony D. Smith, "Gastronomy or Geology? The Role of Nationalism in the Reconstruction of Nations," *Nations and Nationalism* 1, no. 1 (1994): 18–19.

6. There are some free riders too, and people who feel their nation should be otherwise represented. Hence the fact that a nation is formed does not mean that the debate ends; in fact it is only starting.

7. Ernest Renan, "What Is a Nation?," in *Nation and Narration*, ed. Homi K. Bhabha (London: Routledge, 1990), 8–22.

8. Renan, "What Is a Nation?"

9. The story first appears in Mason L. Weems, *The Life of Washington the Great: Enriched with a Number of Very Curious Anecdotes, Perfectly in Character, and Equally Honorable to Himself, and Exemplary to His Young Countrymen* (Augusta, GA: George P. Randolph, 1806).

10. Virginia S. Thatcher, ed., *The New Webster Encyclopedic Dictionary of the English Language* (Chicago: Consolidated Book Publishers, 1980), 180.

11. Benedict Anderson, *Imagined Communities* (London: Verso, 1983), 6.

12. Anderson, *Imagined Communities*, 46.

Chapter 8: National Creativity

1. Milan Kundera, "Die Weltliteratur: European Novelists and Modernism," *New Yorker*, January 8, 2007.

2. Milan Kundera, *The Book of Laughter and Forgetting* (Harmondsworth: Penguin, 1980), 229.

3. Anthony Smith, *National Identity* (Reno: University of Nevada Press, 1991), 160.

4. William Shakespeare, *Henry V*, in *The Complete Works*, ed. W. J. Craig (London: Magpie Books, 1993), 491. Although this text was written in a prenational era, it has been used repeatedly in later periods to arouse national feelings and foster national commitments.

5. Winston Churchill, in a speech delivered in the House of Commons, June 18, 1940.

6. Ernest Renan, *Qu'est-ce que c'est une nation?* (Paris: Colmann Lévy, 1882), 27.

7. Benedict Anderson, *Imagined Communities* (London: Verso, 1983), 201.

8. Anderson, *Imagined Communities*.

9. Shlomo Zand, introduction to Eric Hobsbawm, *Nations and Nationalism since 1780* (Tel Aviv: Resling Press, 1990), 8 (Hebrew—my translation).

10. Milan Kundera, *Identity* (New York: HarperCollins, 1997), 45–46.

Chapter 9: This Place We Call Home

1. Eric J. Hobsbawm, *Nations and Nationalism since 1780: Program, Myth, Reality* (Cambridge: Cambridge University Press, 1999), 92.

2. Yuli (Yael) Tamir, *Liberal Nationalism* (Princeton, NJ: Princeton University Press, 1993), chapter 5: "The Magic Pronoun 'MY.'"

3. Conor Cruise O'Brien, "Nationalists and Democrats," *Times Literary Supplement*, August 15, 1991, 29.

4. Benedict Anderson, *Imagined Communities* (London: Verso, 1983), 7.

5. Genesis 11:6–7.

6. Note that the term *ethnocentric*—putting one's ethnic group at the center—implies an acknowledgment that other groups exist in the periphery.

Chapter 10: La Vie Quotidian

1. Michael Billig, *Banal Nationalism* (Thousand Oaks, CA: Sage, 1995).

2. Tom Stoppard, *Arcadia* (London: Faber and Faber, 1993), 25.

3. William Blake, "Jerusalem," 1804.

4. Eric Storm, "The Nationalization of the Domestic Sphere," *Nations and Nationalism* 23, no. 1 (2017): 173–93.

5. Storm, "Nationalization of the Domestic Sphere."

6. Yael Tamir, *Liberal Nationalism* (Princeton, NJ: Princeton University Press, 2003), 90.

Chapter 11: Subjects into Citizens

1. Cited in Christopher J. Lucas, *Our Western Educational Heritage* (New York: Macmillan, 1971), 470.

2. John Stuart Mill, *Thoughts on Parliamentary Reform* (New York: Cosimo Press, 2009), 25.

3. John Stuart Mill, *Three Essays: On Liberty, Representative Government, The Subjection of Women* (Oxford: Oxford University Press, 1975), 284.

4. Andy Green, *Education and State Formation: The Rise of Education Systems in England, France, and the USA* (New York: St. Martin's Press, 1990), 79, cited in Eric M. Uslaner and Bo Rothstein, "The Historical Roots of Corruption: State Building, Economic Inequality, and Mass Education," *Comparative Politics* 48, no. 2 (2016): 230.

5. Elmer H. Wilds and K. V. Lottich, *The Foundations of Modern Education* (New York: Holt, Rinehart, and Winston, 1968), 329.

6. Teaching was never value neutral; it sketched out a narrative, both national and democratic (and sometimes religious). But it was taken to be true—it took almost a century for members of minority groups and other excluded and marginalized citizens to come forward and claim their share of the curriculum.

7. Paul Auster, *Report from the Interior* (New York: Henry Holt, 2013), 56–59.

8. Uslaner and Rothstein, "Historical Roots of Corruption," 230.

9. Cited in Yuli (Yael) Tamir, "United We Stand?," *Studies in Philosophy and Education* 12, no. 1 (1993): 58.

10. Tamir, "United We Stand?"

11. Cited in Paul R. Mendes-Flohr and Jehuda Reinharz, *The Jew in the Modern World* (Oxford: Oxford University Press, 1980), 109.

12. Cited in Tamir, "United We Stand," 63.

13. Johann G. Fichte, *Addresses to the German Nation*, ed. G. A. Kelly (New York: Harper and Row, 1968), 192.

14. Fichte, *Addresses to the German Nation*, 193.

15. Jean-Jacques Rousseau, *Emile* (New York: Basic Books, 1965), 65.

16. Liah Greenfeld, *Nationalism: Five Roads to Modernity* (Cambridge, MA: Harvard University Press, 1992), 487.

Chapter 12: A Short History of the Cross-Class Coalition

1. Ugo Pagano, "Can Economics Explain Nationalism?," in *Nationalism and Rationality*, ed. Albert Berton, Gianluigi Galeotti, Pierre Salmon, and Ronald Wintrobe (Cambridge: Cambridge University Press, 1995), 177.

2. George Bernard Shaw, *Pygmalion: Definitive Text* (London: Methuen, 2008).

3. Shaw, *Pygmalion*.

4. Tom Nairn, *The Break-Up of Britain: Crisis and Neo-Nationalism* (London: New Left Books, 1977), 41.

5. Jean-Marie Guéhenno, *The End of the Nation-State*, trans. Victoria Elliot (Minneapolis: University of Minnesota Press, 1995), xi.

6. Liah Greenfeld, *Nationalism: Five Roads to Modernity* (Cambridge, MA: Harvard University Press, 1992), 487.

7. Peter Baldwin, *The Politics of Social Solidarity: Class Bases of the European Welfare State, 1875–1975* (Cambridge: Cambridge University Press, 2000), 2.

8. Ugo Pagano, "Can Economics Explain Nationalism?," in *Nationalism and Rationality*, ed. A. Breton, G. Galeotti, P. Salmon, and R. Wintrobe (Cambridge: Cambridge University Press, 1995), 186.

9. Josep R. Llobera, *The God of Modernity: The Development of Nationalism in Western Europe* (Oxford: Berg, 1996), 96.

10. Peter Baldwin, *The Politics of Social Solidarity: Class Bases of the European Welfare State* (Cambridge: Cambridge University Press, 1990), 24–25.

11. Baldwin, *Politics of Social Solidarity*, 24–25.

Chapter 13: The Breakdown of the Cross-Class Coalition

1. This is very well demonstrated by Judith Shklar, "Liberalism of Fear," in *Liberalism and the Moral Life*, ed. Nancy L. Rosenblum (Cambridge, MA: Harvard University Press, 1989). See also my paper criticizing Shklar's view: Yuli (Yael) Tamir, "The Land of the Free and the Fearful," *Constellations: An International Journal of Critical and Democratic Theory* 3, no. 3 (1997).

2. Jean-Claude Michéa, *The Realm of Lesser Evil* (Cambridge: Polity Press, 2009), 34.

3. Jean-Marie Guéhenno, *The End of the Nation-State* (Minneapolis: University of Minnesota Press, 1995), xii.

4. Yvonne Roberts, "Marginalized Young Men," in *The Rise and Rise of Meritocracy*, ed. Geoff Dench (Oxford: Blackwell, 2007), 186.

5. Yuli Tamir, "Staying in Control; or, What Do We Really Want Public Education to Achieve?," *Educational Theory* 61 (2011): 395–411.

6. Alan Bloom, *The Closing of the American Mind* (New York: Simon and Schuster, 1987), 27.

7. Arlie Russell Hochschild, *Strangers in Their Own Land: Anger and Mourning on the American Right* (New York: New Press, 2016), 19.

8. Christopher Lasch, *The Revolt of the Elites and the Betrayal of Democracy* (New York: Norton, 1995), 4.

9. Lasch, *Revolt of the Elites and the Betrayal of Democracy*, 5.

10. The mobile classes are obviously diverse. There is a huge difference between those who travel first class to take a job in an international firm and those who crowd beneath the decks of a shaky boat rejected at every port, in other words, between the motivations and fates of refugees, illegal immigrants, guest workers, contract workers, and professionals. However, in most cases the movers are the more able and powerful members of their own societies. In order to escape, seek refuge, immigrate, one needs certain abilities and skills that are not evenly divided. For example, many of the Syrian refugees are members of the middle class who are, on average, younger, healthier, and more educated than those left behind.

11. Lasch, *Revolt of the Elites and the Betrayal of Democracy*, 6.

12. Anna Maria Mayda and Dani Rodrik, "Why Are Some People (and Countries) More Protectionist Than Others?" unpublished paper, 29, http://citeseerx.ist. psu.edu/viewdoc/download?doi=10.1.1.441.3331&rep=rep1&type=pdf.

13. Mayda and Rodrik, "Why Are Some People."

14. Herman E. Daly, "Globalization and Its Discontents," *Philosophy and Public Policy Quarterly* 21, no. 2–3 (2001): 17.

15. When jobs allowing workers to make a decent living are scarce, immigration encourages a redistribution of wealth away from workers who compete with immigrants and toward employers and other users of immigrant services. In his summary of recent publications on immigration, Christopher Jencks claims that immigration has a small effect on the national product but a big effect on the distribution of income: "Under America's current immigration policy, the winners are employers who get cheap labor, skilled workers who pay less for their burgers and nannies, and immigrants themselves. The losers are unskilled America-born workers." Christopher Jencks, "Who Should Get In?" *New York Review of Books* 8, no. 19, November 29, 2001, http://www.nybooks.com/articles/2001/11/29/who-should-get-in/.

Chapter 14: One Nation, Divided, under Stress

1. Eric Hobsbawm, *Nations and Nationalism* (Cambridge: Cambridge University Press, 1990), 38.

2. Thomas Friedman, *The World Is Flat* (New York: Farrar, Straus and Giroux, 2005), 10–11.

3. Peter Temin, *The Vanishing Middle Class: Prejudice and Power in a Dual Economy* (Cambridge, MA: MIT Press, 2017).

4. Lynn Parramore, "America Is Regressing into a Developing Nation for Most People," *Institute of New Economic Thinking*, April 20, 2017, https://www.ineteconom ics.org/perspectives/blog/america-is-regressing-into-a-developing-nation-for-most -people.

5. Tim Wallace, "The Two Americas of 2016," *New York Times*, November 11, 2016, https://www.nytimes.com/interactive/2016/11/16/us/politics/the-two-americas- of-2016.html.

6. John Harris, "The UK Is Now Two Nations Staring across a Political Chasm," *The Guardian*, June 23, 2016, https://www.theguardian.com/commentisfree/2016 /jun/23/united-kingdom-two-nations-political-chasm-left.

7. Alana Semuels, "Poor at 20, Poor for Life," *The Atlantic*, July 12, 2016, https:// www.theatlantic.com/business/archive/2016/07/social-mobility-america /491240/.

8. Ulrich Beck, "Cosmopolitanism: A Critical Theory for the Twenty-First Century," in *The Blackwell Companion to Globalization*, ed. G. Ritzer (Oxford: Blackwell), 105.

Chapter 15: The Elephant in the Room

1. Kari Marie Norgaard, *Living in Denial: Climate Change, Emotions, and Everyday Life* (Cambridge, MA: MIT Press, 2016), 216.

2. Jerry Mander and Edward Goldsmith, eds., *The Case against the Global Economy* (San Francisco: Sierra Club Books, 1996), 5.

3. Peter L. Berger and Samuel P. Huntington, *Many Civilizations: Cultural Diversity in the Contemporary World* (Oxford: Oxford University Press, 2002), 2.

4. The Third International Mathematics and Science Study (TIMSS) was the largest and most ambitious international study of student achievement ever conducted. It was conducted from 1994 to 1995, at five grade levels (third, fourth, seventh, eighth, and twelfth grades) in more than forty countries. Students were tested in mathematics and science. Altogether TIMSS tested and gathered contextual data for more than half a million students and administered questionnaires to thousands of teachers and school principals. The TIMSS results were released in 1996 and 1997 in a series of reports.

5. A survey carried out in the United States among 1,200 young adults between the ages of eighteen and twenty-nine revealed that 39 percent are dependent on the financial support of their parents, 33 percent live with their parents or relatives, 32 percent struggle to balance their budget, and only 16 percent reported living comfortably. The average young American begins his/her adult life with a debt of $21,900, mostly as a result of education costs.

6. This process is not new; it has been gathering momentum in recent years. An examination of the patterns of growth of Asian education systems reveals a fast and constant growth. True, the initial starting point was very low, and there was much to be accomplished. In Japan postsecondary education rose between 1960 and the mid-1990s from 9 percent to 42 percent. In South Korea the increase over the same time period was even more dramatic: from 5 percent to over 50 percent; China and India showed a slower yet steady rate of growth. In the future, these rates will slow down, and education in Asia will reach a plateau similar to that of many Western countries; by then, however, tens of millions of educated professionals will join the global market, and it is not at all clear whether an equivalent number of well-paying jobs will be created.

7. McKinsey Global Institute Report, *Poorer Than Their Parents: Flat or Falling Incomes in Advanced Economies*, 2016, https://www.mckinsey.com/global-themes /employment-and-growth/poorer-than-their-parents-a-new-perspective-on-income -inequality.

8. McKinsey Global Institute Report, *Poorer Than Their Parents*, 8.

9. Sigal Alon, "The Evolution of Class Inequality in Higher Education: Competition, Exclusion, and Adaptation," *American Sociological Review* 74 (2009): 736.

10. William Deresiewicz, *Excellent Sheep: The Miseducation of the American Elite* (New York: Free Press 2014).

11. Michael D. Carr and Emily Wiemers, "The Decline in Lifetime Earnings Mobility in the US: Evidence from Survey-Linked Administrative Data," *Washington Center for Equitable Growth*, April 2016, 1, http://equitablegrowth.org/equitablog/ the-decline-in-lifetime-earnings-mobility-in-the-u-s-evidence-from-survey-linked- administrative-data/.

12. Yuli Tamir, "Staying in Control; or, What Do We Really Want Public Education to Achieve?," *Educational Theory* 61 (2011).

13. James David Vance, *Hillbilly Elegy: A Memoir of a Family and Culture in Crisis* (New York: Harper Collins, 2016), 191.

14. When Vance's father learned that Vance had been admitted to Yale, he asked whether he had pretended to be liberal or black. This, Vance concludes, is how low the cultural expectations of working-class whites have fallen. Vance, *Hillbilly Elegy*, 194.

15. Barack Obama, "Remarks by President Obama in Address to the People of Europe," speech, Hannover, Germany, April 25, 2016, https://ua.usembassy.gov

/remarks-president-obama-address-people-europe/. His last point is a clear reference to Rawls's original position and the global implementation of a veil of ignorance. See John Rawls, *A Theory of Justice* (Oxford: Oxford University Press, 1972).

Chapter 16: The Birth of a Nationalist

1. Tony Blair, "Against Populism, the Center Must Hold," *New York Times*, March 3, 2017, https://www.nytimes.com/2017/03/03/opinion/tony-blair-against-populism-the-center-must-hold.html.

2. Naomi Grimley, "Identity 2016: 'Global Citizenship' Rising, Poll Suggests," *BBC*, April 28, 2016, http://www.bbc.com/news/world-36139904.

3. Thomas Nagel, *Mortal Questions* (Cambridge: Cambridge University Press, 1979), 33–34.

4. Nagel, *Mortal Questions*, 34.

5. John Locke, *Second Treatise of Government*, chapter V, paragraph 33.

6. Positioning oneself at the N pole does not imply resistance to globalism altogether but rather seeing globalism through a national prism. In other words, it expresses a wish that the state will remain a player in the global arena, offering some checks and balances to protect its members. It would therefore be misleading to argue that the conflict between the Gs and the Ns is between a borderless world and a barbed wire one. The difference is one of priorities.

Chapter 17: The Nationalism of the Vulnerable

1. For an excellent example of this discussion see Nancy Fraser and Axel Honneth, *Redistribution or Recognition* (New York: Verso, 2003).

2. Mark Lilla, *The Once and Future Liberal: After Identity Politics* (New York: HarperCollins, 2017), 7.

3. Drafting a curriculum, one soon realizes that there is no such place as "neutrality." In other words, no place is equally distant from all points of view, and all life experiences. Whose story should the school system tell is always at the center of some controversy.

4. James David Vance, *Hillbilly Elegy: A Memoir of a Family and Culture in Crisis* (New York: Harper Collins, 2016), 189.

5. Arlie Russell Hochschild, *Strangers in Their Own Land: Anger and Mourning on the American Right* (New York: New Press, 2016).

6. Vance, *Hillbilly Elegy*, 134–35 (according to the 2016 McKinsey report, members of all groups overestimate the chance of their children being better off than their parents).

7. Vance, *Hillbilly Elegy*, 134–35.

8. David K. Shipler, *The Working Poor: Invisible in America* (New York: Vintage Books, 2004), 5–6.

9. Graham Whitham, "Challenging 12 Myths and Stereotypes about Low Income Families and Social Security," *Save the Children*, November 2012.

10. Adam Roberts, "Humour Is a Funny Thing," *Journal of Aesthetics* 56, no. 4 (2016).

11. Vance, *Hillbilly Elegy*.

12. Hochschild, *Strangers in Their Own Land*, 32.

13. Vance, *Hillbilly Elegy*, 3.

14. Vance, *Hillbilly Elegy*, 236.

15. Selina Todd, *The People: The Rise and Fall of the Working Class* (London: John Murray, 2014), 243.

16. Joseph E. Stiglitz, *The Principle of Inequality: How Today's Divided Society Endangers Our Future* (New York: Norton, 2012), 233.

17. Stiglitz, *Principle of Inequality*, 225.

18. See the interesting debate that followed the Supreme Court decision that followed *Regents of the University of California v. Bakke*, 438 U.S. 265 (1978).

19. Mike Savage, "The 'Class Ceiling' and the New Class War," *The Guardian*, October 22, 2015, https://www.theguardian.com/books/2015/oct/22/new-class-war-politics-class-just-beginning.

20. For an extensive discussion of this issue see Yuli Tamir, "Staying in Control; or, What Do We Really Want Public Education to Achieve?," *Educational Theory* 61 (2011).

21. In an insightful book describing the way poverty shapes human life, Sendhil Mullainathan and Eldar Shafir explain how extreme social conditions influence the way people think and act. They claim that the poor not only have less opportunities but are also less able to take advantage of the opportunities they have. With scarcity in mind, they have less mind for everything else. Sendhil Mullainathan and Eldar Shafir, *Scarcity: Why Having Too Little Means So Much* (New York: Times Books, 2013), 157.

22. BBC News, "Brexit: Reaction from around the UK," June 24, 2016, http://www.bbc.com/news/uk-politics-eu-referendum-36619444.

23. Dani Rodrik, *The Globalization Paradox* (Oxford: Oxford University Press, 2011), xix.

Chapter 18: The Nationalism of the Affluent

1. Ernest Gellner, *Nations and Nationalism* (Oxford: Blackwell, 1983), 45.

2. Most of Europe's smaller states were either established in an earlier period—the Netherlands was defined as an independent political unit in 1648 at the end of the Eighty Years' War and turned into a parliamentary democracy in 1846; Switzerland was

acknowledged as an independent state after the Peace of Westphalia in 1648; Luxembourg gained independence from France in 1815—or following the collapse of the Soviet Union: Latvia gained independence in 1991 alongside Lithuania and Estonia. The breakup of Yugoslavia also created four small states: Macedonia, Bosnia, Serbia, and Montenegro.

3. Friedrich List as cited in Eric Hobsbawm, *Nations and Nationalism* (Cambridge: Cambridge University Press, 1990), 30–31.

4. Hobsbawm, *Nations and Nationalism*, 30.

5. Gellner, *Nations and Nationalism*, 48.

6. John Stuart Mill, *Utilitarianism, Liberty, and Representative Government* (Oxford: Oxford University Press, 2015), 363–64.

7. The Spanish Constitution, Section II.

8. Stephan Burgen, "Fictional Catalan Region of Tabarnia Appoints First President," *The Guardian*, January 16, 2018.

9. Steven Erlanger, "For E.U., Catalonian Pits Democratic Rights against Sovereignty," *New York Times*, October 2, 2017, https://www.nytimes.com/2017/10/02/world/europe/catalonia-independence-referendum-eu.html.

Chapter 19: Liberal Nationalism

1. Dani Rodrik, "Who Needs the Nation State," *Economic Geometry*, 89, no. 1 (2012): 3.

2. Salvatore Settis, *If Venice Dies* (New York: New Vessel Press, 2017).

3. Ivan Krastev, *After Europe* (Philadelphia: University of Pennsylvania Press, 2017), 25.

4. Emmanuel Macron, public speech, 2017, https://books.google.co.il/books?id=6qdFDwAAQBAJ&pg=PA209&lpg=PA209&dq=When+I+look+at+Marseille,+I+see+a+French+city,+shaped+by+two+thousand+years+of+history,+or+immigration,+of+Europe&source=bl&ots=L9xu-fvpD5&sig=I8YDwdGb3_Pz-RqY94O-FAi7Lo4c&hl=en&sa=X&ved=oahUKEwjvgqj36sjbAhVpCsAKHToHCd8Q6AEIJzAA#v=onepage&q=When%20I%20look%20at%20Marseille%2C%20I%20see%20a%20French%20city%2C%20shaped%20by%20two%20thousand%20years%20of%20history%2C%20or%20immigration%2C%20of%20Europe&f=false..

5. Phil Hoad, "Corrupt, Dangerous, and Brutal to Its Poor—Is Marseille the Future of France? *The Guardian*, June 8, 2017.

6. Rory Smith and Elian Peltier, "Kylian Mbappé and the Boys from the Banlieues," *New York Times*, July 6, 2018.

7. Jacques Barou, *Integration of Immigrants in France: A Historical Perspective*, Identities: Global Studies in Culture and Power (Routledge), vol. 6, December 2014, 647.

8. Barou, *Integration of Immigrants*.

9. Matthias Bartsch, Andrea Brandt, and Daniel Steinvorth, "Turkish Immigration to Germany: A Sorry History of Self-Deception and Wasted Opportunities," *Spiegel*, September 7, 2010.

10. Joachim Bottner, "How the Far Right Conquered Sweden," *New York Times*, September, 6, 2018.

11. Yascha Mounk, *The People vs. Democracy: Why Our Freedom Is in Danger and How to Save It* (Cambridge, MA: Harvard University Press, 2018), 208.

12. Mounk *People vs. Democracy*, 167.

13. Carol A. Larsen, "Revitalizing the 'Civic' and 'Ethnic' Distinction: Perceptions of Nationhood across Two Dimensions, 44 Countries, and Two Decades," *Nations and Nationalism* 23, no. 4 (2017).

14. Larsen, "Revitalizing the 'Civic' and 'Ethnic' Distinction," 989.

15. Krastev, *After Europe* 40.

Chapter 20: This Is the Time

1. Credit Suisse Research Institute, "Global Wealth Report" (Zurich: Credit Suisse, 2017), 27, https://www.poder360.com.br/wp-content/uploads/2017/11/global-wealth-report-2017-en.pdf.

2. Arlie Russell Hochschild, *Strangers in Their Own Land: Anger and Mourning on the American Right* (New York: New Press, 2016), 150.

Chapter 21: A Race to the Bottom

1. "A Conversation with Mark Lilla on His Critique of Identity Politics," *New Yorker*, August 25, 2017, https://www.newyorker.com/news/news-desk/a-conversation-with-mark-lilla-on-his-critique-of-identity-politics.

2. Martha Nussbaum, *Political Emotions: Why Love Matters for Justice* (Cambridge, MA: Harvard University Press, 2013), 346.

3. Nussbaum, *Political Emotions*, 351.

4. Andrew Wroe, "Economic Insecurity and Political Trust in the United States," *America Politics Research* 44, no. 1 (2016): 131–63.

5. Tom W. G. Van der Meer, "Political Trust and the Crisis of Democracy," in *Oxford Research Encyclopedia of Politics*, ed. William R. Thompson (New York: Oxford University Press, 2016).

6. Bernie Sanders, "Bernie's Announcement," May 26, 2015, https://berniesanders.com/bernies-announcement/.

7. Theresa May, speech to Conservative Party Conference, October 2016, http://www.mirror.co.uk/news/uk-news/theresa-mays-speech-conservative-party-8983265.

8. May, speech.

9. Alexandria Ocasio-Cortez: https://www.haaretz.co.il/news/world/america/. premium-1.6218281?utm_source=App_Share&utm_medium=iOS_Native.

10. Christine Emba, "Elizabeth Warren Is Giving Capitalism the Moral Rub It Needs," *Washington Post*, August 30, 2018.

11. *The Economist*, "Britain's Political Centre of Gravity Is Moving Left," Economist Staff, August 25, 2018.

12. *The Economist*, "Britain's Political Centre."

13. For an elaborate analysis of this kind of nationalism, see Yael (Yuli) Tamir, *Liberal Nationalism* (Princeton, NJ: Princeton University Press, 2003).

14. Isaiah Berlin, *Four Essays on Liberty* (Oxford: Oxford University Press, 1969), 172.

Index

15; of everyday life, 72–75; as a
fabrication that helps in coping
with the world, 48; liberalism,
democracy, and, xvi, 6; making the
case for, 23–24; Marxist argument
regarding, 89–90; modernization
and, 27–29; as the moral option,
170–71; the national narrative and
(*see* national narrative); Nazism and
fascism as most extreme expression
of, 22; negative descriptions of,
26–27, 29–31; particularization,
fulfilling the task of, 54; polycentric
distinguished from ethnocentric,
71; populism and, 29–31; rebuilding
a cross-class coalition based on,
166–68; reemergence of, 3–5, 10–11;
taming the new, 178–80, 178–81;
territorial element of, 35–36 (*see
also* borders); two forms of
present-day, 8–10 (*see also* nationalism of the affluent/separatism;
nationalism of the vulnerable); the
universality of particularism in,
68–71; as working class reaction to
elites' globalism, 100–101
Nationalism: Five Roads to Modernity
(Greenfeld), 28
nationalism of the affluent/separatism:
conditions leading to, 142; current
examples of, 143, 146–51; small
nations and the state integrity
argument, 148–50; small nations
and the threshold argument,
143–45; success of, potential for,
150–51; utilitarian arguments,
insufficiency of, 145–48
nationalism of the vulnerable, 9–10;
conditions leading to, 127–31;

divisive effects of opportunities
and risks, 168–69; electoral
consequences of, 135, 138–39; poor
whites and, plight of, 131–35; in the
reemergence of nationalism, 177;
revival of nationalism, 140–41;
victory of the elites and, 135–38
national liberation, second wave of, 18
national narrative: creativity and the
transgenerational context provided
by, 61–62; national sciences
recruited to support, 66; nation
building and, 54–57, 60; question-
ing of in academic institutions, 128;
as remembrance and forgetfulness,
64–67
nation building: education and (*see*
education); national/collective
consciousness and the boundaries
of the nation, 58–60; nationalism
as all-encompassing power in,
52–53; the national narrative and,
54–57, 60
nation-state, the: as alliance of nation
and state, 52; arguments for larger
vs. smaller nation-states, 143–45,
148; benefits guaranteed by, 87–89;
borders and the territorial element
of, 35–36 (*see also* borders); as the
caring state, 53; the cross-class
coalition in, 86–90; demise of, 7–8;
forward-looking goals of, 29;
globalism and (*see* globalism); as
homelands, 40, 69–71; individualist
nature of globalism as threat to,
102–4; intervention by, necessity of,
167–68; liberal democracy and
nationalism, as meeting place of, 6;
liberalism and, 53–54; multinational